networked
theology

Engaging Culture

William A. Dyrness and Robert K. Johnston, series editors

The Engaging Culture series is designed to help Christians respond with theological discernment to our contemporary culture. Each volume explores particular cultural expressions, seeking to discover God's presence in the world and to involve readers in sympathetic dialogue and active discipleship. These books encourage neither an uninformed rejection nor an uncritical embrace of culture, but active engagement informed by theological reflection.

networked theology

negotiating faith in digital culture

heidi a. campbell
and stephen garner

B
BakerAcademic
a division of Baker Publishing Group
Grand Rapids, Michigan

Published by Baker Academic
a division of Baker Publishing Group
P.O. Box 6287, Grand Rapids, MI 49516-6287
www.bakeracademic.com

Printed in the United States of America

Library of Congress Cataloging-in-Publication Data

Names: Campbell, Heidi, 1970– author. | Garner, St. (Stephen) author.
Title: Networked theology : negotiating faith in digital culture / Heidi A. Campbell and Stephen Garner.
Description: Grand Rapids, MI : Baker Academic, a division of Baker Publishing Group, [2016] | Series: Engaging culture | Includes bibliographical references and index.
Identifiers: LCCN 2016017643 | ISBN 9780801049149 (pbk.)
Subjects: LCSH: Mass media in religion. | Mass media—Religious aspects—Christianity. | Digital media—Religious aspects—Christianity. | Digital communications—Religious aspects—Christianity. | Social media—Religious aspects—Christianity.
Classification: LCC BV652.95 .C36 2016 | DDC 261.5/2—dc23
LC record available at https://lccn.loc.gov/2016017643

In keeping with biblical principles of creation stewardship, Baker Publishing Group advocates the responsible use of our natural resources. As a member of the Green Press Initiative, our company uses recycled paper when possible. The text paper of this book is composed in part of post-consumer waste.

For Kim, Mark, Chris,
Laura, and Philip
and
in memory of
Vivian Margaret Campbell,
who loved theology!

contents

acknowledgments

Heidi A. Campbell wishes to thank the Vaughan Park Scholars Scheme in New Zealand and John Fairbrother, who provided me with space in the fall of 2009 where I began to envision this book project and where Stephen and I first began our conversations on theology and technology. Since that time my thinking on theology and new media has been greatly informed and enriched by insightful conversation with a number of theologians and religion and media scholars around the world—namely, Lynne Baab, Tim Bulkley, Michael Delashmutt, John Dyer, Mary Hess, Peter Horsfield, Tim Hutchings, Miranda Klaver, Paul Soukup, Matthew Tan, and Pete Ward. I am also grateful to the University of Durham COFUND Scheme at the Institute for Advanced Study, especially Simon Litchfield, and to CODEC at St John's College, especially David Wilkinson, who hosted me in fall 2012 as a visiting senior scholar. It was then that initial drafts of many of my chapters were mapped out in the inspiring environments of Bex Lewis's lounge, East Coast and Cross Country trains as I traversed the UK, and Flat White in Durham, where I pondered over many a cuppa. Very special thanks go out to Andy Byers, Bex Lewis, Pete Phillips, and Byrony Taylor from CODEC, who read and provided useful comments on early drafts of my chapters. I am further blessed by my international friendship and family network—including John Campbell, Nicola Hoggard-Creegan, Heather and Robb Elmatti, Gigi and John Greene, John and Sally Stuart, Helen and David Senior, and Judy Webster—who have supported me through this writing project and provided me with food, feedback, and encouragement along the way. Thanks also to my coauthor, Stephen Garner, for being a committed discussion partner and collaborator; to Kathy DiSanto, my faithful friend and copyeditor; and to Robert Hosack at Baker Publishing for his patience and oversight in this project.

Stephen Garner is thankful for the many conversations about faith and technology over the years leading up to this book project. Some of these conversations came out of the computer science communities I studied and worked in, pricking my interest in situating technology within the context of Christian faith. I am particularly indebted to Tony Smith at the University of Waikato, Hamilton, for early conversations in this area. I am also grateful for the support and encouragement I received from the theology faculty at the University of Auckland in terms of early research funding and the companionship of Elaine Wainwright, Nick Thompson, and Caroline Blyth. More recently, I am indebted to my current employer, Laidlaw College, and to Martin Sutherland and Tim Meadowcroft for their ongoing support as friends and colleagues. I would also like to thank the students I have taught in theology, technology, and media courses for their questions that got right to the heart of networked theology. My work has also been influenced and enriched by many conversations with Australasian theologians and media scholars, including Tim Bulkeley, Steve Taylor, Craig Mitchell, Ann Hardy, Peter Horsfield, Paul Emerson Teusner, and Lynne Baab. Others along the way, such as Jason Clark, Bex Lewis, Mary Hess, and Andrew Bradstock, have added their voices to the conversations. To Heidi Campbell, my coauthor, my deep thanks for our many conversations and collaborations on media and theology over the years and for your hard work in steering this project. I am blessed by your scholarship and friendship. To my wife, Kim, and children, Mark, Chris, Laura, and Philip, thank you for all your love and for the time given to this project. Finally, thanks to Kathy DiSanto for her copyediting and to Robert Hosack at Baker Publishing for his ongoing support for this project.

introduction

When New Media Meets Faith

We live in a world where our digital technologies are increasingly intersecting with our spiritual lives. This is not only changing personal presentations of faith—as blogs, podcasts, and social media become important public platforms for individuals to discuss their beliefs—but also the way we do church. The Barna Research Group reported significant increases in church leaders' use of the internet (from 78 percent in 2000 to 97 percent in 2014), especially for information gathering, keeping up existing relationships, and making new friends. It also noted an increase in pastors' perception of the internet as useful for facilitating spiritual or religious experiences (from 15 percent to 39 percent). In 2014 nine out of ten pastors believed that it is "theologically acceptable for a church to provide faith assistance or religious experiences to people through the Internet." Overall, many churches in America viewed the internet as having moved from being a luxury to being an essential tool for ministry.[1]

The Church of England announced plans in early 2015 to equip all of its sixteen thousand churches with Wi-Fi internet access to draw more visitors to these sites and encourage churches to enhance and develop outreach programs to serve the practical and spiritual needs of a digital generation.[2] As the internet increasingly becomes a place where people meet and live a large portion of their social lives, the call has been sounded ever louder to meet them there with the gospel of Christ. In 2014 the Billy Graham Evangelistic Association recorded over six million online conversions connected to their website and resources, in contrast to only fifteen thousand converts made through face-to-face outreach.[3] Similarly, Global Media Outreach—a ministry that leverages the internet, mobile devices, and social media—claimed that more than thirty-four million people made decisions to follow Christ through its digital evangelization work.[4]

Technological innovations give rise to experimentation with new forms of creative outreach and religious education and discipleship resources. For instance, Christian technology developers and workers with the American Bible Society have pondered how Microsoft's new holographic technology and augmented reality goggles such as Oculus Rift might be used to superimpose digital text on interactive images of Bible passages, opening the way for a holographic Bible and study materials.[5] Other trends in digital ministry include e-giving, which provides members with online and mobile giving options though touch-screen kiosks and mobile apps, and virtual world churches, which use virtual-reality technology to create digital worship experiences in online environments for avatar-based worshipers.[6]

As digital media continue to find a way into church practice and our everyday lives, we are increasingly faced with the challenge of how to evaluate and theologically reflect on these changes. We, the authors, believe that theological discourse must be taken seriously to understand how new media shape our everyday lives and the ethical impact of our technological engagement on our perception of what it means to be human. Such reflection requires moving beyond the overly simplistic framing of technology as either good or evil. Some current work on the church and the internet has focused on how digital media can or should be used in worship or ministry contexts, presenting digital media as tools simply to be embraced for the cause of Christ. Other work has sought to offer a general Christian appraisal of the nature and impact of technologies on the church and society, but it has started with the assumption that media technologies are all-powerful and users are passive respondents to media's influence. This work has framed technology as inherently problematic, always promoting values that need to be resisted by the faithful.

While many books have sought to offer a Christian theological reflection on digital technologies, few have presented clear, systematic investigations that not only allow readers to reflect deeply on how the characteristics of new media correlate with emerging social practice but also provide concrete resources for evaluating the theological trajectory created by new media values. This book starts with the assumption that any analysis of religious approaches to new media involves a careful reading of technological trends within our global information society, coupled with a Christian ethical analysis of media grounded in a thoughtful theology of technology. This book seeks to map out and provide readers with a framework for identifying an authentic theology of new media that relates to their faith communities.

We offer the concept of *networked theology* as a way to describe our approach to theologizing about the digital, technological, and network society in which we live. Networked theology draws together discourse in media theory on the nature of how communication networks are conceived and function. It stresses that within digital culture our relationships with information and others have changed from static, controlled structures to dynamic, adaptive connections. The network represents a unique form of social relations that is reshaping how people see and interact with others. The culture created by networks has important theological implications and challenges for how we treat the other around us and connected to us. We thus turn to the resources offered within theological discourse on technology to see how the Christian tradition can guide our response to these new relationships and patterns of interaction. Later in this introduction we will unpack this approach to theology. For now we note that networked theology offers a useful and important conceptual image for how the internet, as the network of networks, offers a unique and vibrant space calling us to new forms of theological inquiry. Such inquiry can help us contextualize and explain the life of faith in the twenty-first century.

In the pages that follow, we set out a systematic analysis through a series of conversation points on how people of faith consume and are affected by digital media. This leads to focused discussion of the effects that these technologies and their traits can have on our social and spiritual lives and what theological resources can be of use in our technological discernment process. This introduction begins with a discussion of the complex relationship between new media, faith, and digital culture. We argue that new media technologies are situated in a unique cultural context, described by scholars as the network society, that frames how we understand the social world and raises important theological issues for people of faith. This leads to a detailed reflection on the metaphor of the network and our understanding of theology. We present the idea of networked theology as a framework for understanding the intersection between new media and theology. After introducing these key concepts, we outline the contents and trajectory of the rest of the book.

The Nature of the Network in Network Society

The network has become a popular and powerful metaphor in digital culture. It offers a dynamic image to portray how the internet functions, the nature of social interactions online, and the infrastructure supporting our information-based society. Indeed, many have argued that we now live in a network society, in which new social, economic, political, and cultural structures are emerging from an increasingly wired and global world. Because the network has become an important framing concept, we must unpack the assumptions and expectations embedded within this image to see how they affect our understanding of doing theology within this context. To do this, we will briefly consider three important discourses from which certain beliefs about the nature of networks emerge. These discourses come from (1) science fiction and stories related to the birth of the internet, (2) the rise of social network analysis as a new way to understand contemporary communities, and (3) rhetoric related to the network society. By discussing the image of the network in each of these contexts, we will discover some significant assumptions about how society functions, how people interrelate, and how dominant cultural values emerge that shape people's expectations and behaviors in the new media landscape.

The Network in Science Fiction and Nonfiction

The image of the network is arguably connected to the birth of the term "cyberspace." Coined by William Gibson in his classic science-fiction novel *Neuromancer*, the term was used to describe a computer-generated space in a near-future world where most of earth's computers have been connected in a global network. People entered this network through "a virtual-reality grid space" known as cyberspace, a technical and yet human network. Cyberspace became an idea used to encapsulate the notion of a wired space connecting humans to a computer-created world. As a network connecting humans and machines, it became a popular image within science-fiction films of the 1980s and 1990s. The network was presented as everything from a space of entrapment to one of ultimate freedom—from *Tron*'s (Disney, 1982) circuit-board world inside the mainframe computer where programs battled for their very existence to the *Matrix* trilogy's (Warner Bros., 1999 and 2003) dystopic future in which humanity was enslaved by an all-encompassing network of sentient machines. The matrix was a simulated reality implanted in human consciousness by the machines to keep humans complacent about this system as humans functioned as passive batteries powering the network. More recent films such as *Transcendence* (Alcon Entertainment, 2013) and *Her* (Annapurna Pictures, 2013) feature similar story lines that present computer networks as spaces that give life to sentient artificial intelligences seeking to control or deceive humanity. In all of these narratives, the network represents both promise and peril. Within these computer networks lies a sense of hope for a better world that empowers humans with unique abilities and potential, mingled with an overarching sense of hopelessness that our technologies will ultimately overpower and control us.

This tension—between utopian possibilities that the technological world offers and a possible dystopic future reality created by a computer-controlled environment—is heightened by the rhetoric surrounding the rise of the internet. The network became an important metaphor to describe the function and capture the innovative nature of the internet in the mid-1990s. One of the earliest precursors of today's internet was ARPANET, launched in 1969 by the Advanced Research Projects Agency (ARPA), a division of the US Department of Defense, as a government-funded research-sharing tool. Over a twenty-five-year period, this early computer network grew from a resource accessible only to researchers associated with the defense industry to a collaborative tool used by the wider scientific community, which was eager to have access to the revolutionary possibilities offered in data sharing and cooperation. By the early 1990s, the internet was defined as "a collection of over two thousand packet switched networks" located worldwide.[7]

"Internet" is a shortening of "internetworking," a term referring to the connecting of smaller computer networks such as local area networks (LANs) through a series of links—known as gateways—that help route and transfer information through an interconnected system of computers. By the time the internet became a public entity in the United States in 1996, it networked a variety of software and services, including the World Wide Web (WWW). The internet provided unique opportunities for information access and exchange. Soon the public and the popular press began to refer to the internet as "the web" or "the net," terms that seemed to capture the way individuals actually interacted with this new technology, moving in a nonlinear fashion from webpage to webpage and creating their own nonhierarchical networks of interactions. Even Microsoft in its 1998 version of Windows opted to replace its initial desktop metaphor with the icons and symbolism of a network.

These images of the internet as a network echoed some of the hype surrounding the internet at the time. The internet was presented as a space connecting people to endless opportunities for education, social interaction, and freedom of information. The image of the network also promoted a decentralized view of control, promoting a flattening of hierarchical structures and allowing people to share and connect in ways not before possible. In a network, interactions can begin from a variety of points or perspectives rather than one central control or gatekeeper. This means that information can travel from one point to another on multiple paths, offering people new and flexible options for connecting. Thus, people talked about the internet as contributing to the redefinition of traditional boundaries. For example, in the mid-1990s Bill Gates, in his book *The Road Ahead*, speculated that the internet would change our patterns of socialization and systems of education, forcing us to rethink the nature of our relationships. He stated, "The network will draw us together, if that's what we choose, or let us scatter ourselves into a million mediated communities. Above all, and in countless new ways, the information highway will give us choices that can put us in touch with entertainment, information, and each other."[8] Cyber-philosophers in the 1990s and early 2000s, from Mark Numes to Donna Haraway, used the image of the network to discuss the potential for redefining traditional power and gender relations. They believed the internet would provide an opportunity to reenvision social structure, class, and race relations, creating a space where the voices of the previously marginalized could be heard.

The image of the network continues to be associated with the internet as a way to talk about how the internet functions, as a space of information exchange, and as a platform for new social and cultural interactions. The image acts as both a conceptual tool and a metaphoric reality. Its previous connection to science-fiction narratives highlights a core assumption: that the network represents a space where human and machine merge in a new relationship that can lead either to hopeful escape from the constraints of the physical world or to a place of technological domination and control.

The Network in Social Network Analysis

The internet has been popularly framed as a social network, a place of unlimited connections where, through a few clicks or links, people find themselves interacting with others and not just searching for information. The social nature of the internet has also been key to its development. ARPANET, the predecessor of the current internet, was established as a research-sharing platform. The birth of email in 1970 soon transformed the network into a message system and social interchange, and email became the dominant use of the internet for over three decades.[9] Using the internet as a sphere of social connection became even more popular with innovations such as email lists, bulletin board services, and newsgroups that allowed network users to interact with one another by posting messages and, later, through asynchronous platforms such as chat rooms and multi-user dimensions (MUDs). Early internet researchers such as Steve Jones observed that, for many, the internet is primarily a social landscape, "because it is made by people and thus as the 'new public space' it conjoins traditional mythic narratives of progress with the strong modern impulses towards self-fulfillment and personal development."[10] In an age of social media, tendencies to use internet technologies to socialize, maintain relationships, play games, and receive emotional support have become even more prevalent.

This framing of the internet as a social network is not just a practical distinction; it is rooted in a larger theoretical framework touching on shifts occurring within society. Beginning in the 1950s, sociologists began to document changes in the nature of community. Drawing on the work of German sociologist Ferdinand Tönnies, who first observed a cultural shift from tightly bound community relationships to loose societal associations within rural and urban settings in the nineteenth century, sociologists of community began to observe changes within the structure of society. Modern society, instead of being made up of homogeneous, small-scale relationship networks defined by geographical and familial relations, was marked by fluid boundaries, changing interactions, and diverse, large-scale associations based on needs. Community studies began to focus on how people created social structures in vast urban spaces where loosely bound interpersonal relationships were the norm.[11]

This understanding within sociology of community studies helped birth social network analysis. This new approach to the study of community argues that communities are in their essence social structures and not spatial or geographic structures such as neighborhoods. Social network analysis is a method used to identify a set of nodes (which can be persons, groups, or organizations) and the ties between all or some of them in order to understand the social structures that emerge from the network of relationships. Proponents of this approach argue that communities are best understood as dynamic, changeable, self-selecting structures that create networks defined by commonality and select needs or interests. This is a very different view of community, which is traditionally defined by familial, institutional, and other tightly bounded relations.

The internet provided a unique environment for studying new forms of community, and sociologists were quick to use social network analysis as a way to approach and document how relationships function online. Barry Wellman argued in his essay "An Electronic Group Is Virtually a Social Network" that online discussion forums could be described as communities representing a network of free-form relationships that are constantly changing and resist being tied down.[12] Social network analysis has been used to map the shape and composition of community networks existing online, to study the strength of different social ties within a given network, and to observe how networks relate to or influence one another. Online communities, as they represented a group of people culturing a new technological and social space together in a new social context, presented a new way to explore changing social relations in contemporary society. Although in the 1990s and early 2000s studies portraying community as a social network were often seen as employing a controversial or debatable depiction, today that image has become mainstream. The network metaphor has become an important frame for describing not only the function of online communities but also the nature of community offline.

The framing of community as a network supports a number of assumptions about social relationships: they are fluid and based on changeable connections that vary in depth, and they promote individual choice, malleability, and dynamic interactions.[13] The network in this sense is social, but it facilitates community through personally regulated, specialized association, encouraging individual choice over corporate cohesion and accountability.

The Network in the Network Society

We cannot fully understand thinking and assumptions about networks without also discussing the network society. This conceptual framework is used by scholars to describe the social structure that has emerged from the proliferation and integration of new information technologies in society. The term "network society" was coined by Dutch media sociologist Jan van Dijk to describe the new form of society he saw developing.[14] According to van Dijk, the increasing integration of global, business, interpersonal, and media networks in many areas of society in the late 1980s and early 1990s gave rise to a unique social structure in which information and its exchange became the central economic commodity.

Manuel Castells discusses the idea of a network society in his work on the information age.[15] He argues that there is a shift in understanding of how social, political, and economic worlds function in globalized society. This social-technical infrastructure creates a network-based society where social relations are increasingly decentralized yet interconnected. Castells is concerned with the impact that this internationalized information economy has on systems of labor, production, and power. In other words, the network creates new systems that privilege the process and structures of the network over the actual content or information that networks exchange. Castells argues that the process of networking is creating a network economy and networked organizations with actors who depend on each other for information and support. The network substructure pervades all areas of society, exemplified by the increasing dependence on the infrastructure of the internet, where interpersonal, organizational, and mass communication come together to support new levels of social and economic interaction.

For Castells and others, the logic of the network is seen to pervade much of contemporary society, becoming a powerful force shaping how we think about our business, civic, and even personal relationships. This logic is one of dichotomies and tensions. The network both unites people and fragments them into specialized groups; it promotes both collaboration and individuation. The network is a social environment that builds a new space that both draws together and excludes. The network has also become the dominant metaphor for describing the expectation and patterns of behavior for how people interrelate within our information-based society. This argument is articulated by Lee Raine and Barry Wellman in *Networked: The New Social Operating System*, in which they suggest that the network has become the model and logic by which society functions.[16] Wellman has long suggested that societies are best understood as networks of flexible social relations rather than bound groups embedded in hierarchical structures. In *Networked*, Wellman and Raine assert that the social-technical infrastructure of the internet and mobile technologies has transformed the ways we connect to one another and thus our expectations for how we learn, provide support, and make decisions. They describe this social operating system of the network as "networked individualism" marked by several core characteristics: "The social operating system is *personal*—the individual is at the autonomous center just as she is reaching out from her computer; *multiuser*—people are interacting with numerous diverse others; *multitasking*—people are doing several things; and *multithreaded*—they are doing them more or less simultaneously."[17]

A benefit of networked individualism is that it encourages active participation and exchange with others in the network. Examples of this are crowdsourcing, problem solving via blogging, and maintaining valued social relations through mediated connections (e.g., Facebook) that can strengthen physically separated family and friendship tribes. However, such networked individualism also encourages loose, fragmented networks of relationships and can enable individuals to develop multiple social circles rather than investing and being accountable to a single group. This creates a situation where "people function more as connected individuals and less as embedded group members."[18] Thus, the network in the network society is a distinctive social system undergirded by digital communication technologies that promote new forms of social connection and information sharing and encourage individual choice and freedom.

Summarizing the Network Metaphor

This brief survey of the network metaphor provides some important insights into assumptions carried within this image. The network is embedded with both positive and negative narratives, offering us hope for a better future through technology, along with the seeds of fear that our technologies will seduce or enslave us. Networking offers opportunities that can simultaneously connect and divide us. Thus, the network is a social system that privileges the individual in ways that can either encourage innovative interactions and relationship building or lead to possibly isolating patterns of being.

The network has become an important conceptual tool to describe the ways that people in contemporary society interact and build community. In many respects, seeing community as a network offers us a more accurate picture of how people form and maintain relationships, including relationships within religious contexts.[19] Nancy Ammerman suggests in her study of Christian congregations that many churches function as a network of social relations and that the recognition of this can strengthen the role and influence of churches in modern community life.[20] Therefore, the network not only offers us a useful metaphor for describing contemporary social life and relations but also contains values that are both promising and potentially problematic for communities of faith.

Defining Theology

The term "theology," derived from the Greek words *theos* (god) and *logos* (word or teaching or study), literally means "words about god" or "the teaching about or study of god."[21] In Christianity the understanding of what constitutes theology and how it is approached has developed over time, yet Christian theology remains focused on the figure of Jesus of Nazareth, seeking to understand and articulate both his identity and his work in restoring the relationship of people and the wider world with God.

In the eleventh century, Anselm of Canterbury (c. 1033–1109) described theology as "faith seeking understanding" (Latin: *fides querens intellectum*). Anselm's approach, often used as a starting point for defining Christian theology, emphasizes the need for believers to intelligently seek to comprehend how the study of God should be applied and worked out in the context in which they find themselves. Anselm's definition was rooted in his own medieval context and so suggests that every generation must rearticulate what theology is in relation to the sociocultural situation of its day. Thus, theology is an active pursuit of making meaning of the world through the eyes of faith.

This human desire for meaning-making results from lived experience in the world or an encounter with God. People, individually or as a community, seek to narrate their experiences in a way that helps them make sense of life and locate themselves in a wider story that connects them with God, with others, and with the wider world. In doing this, people move from what Neil Darragh calls *implicit* theology, an automatic response shaped by values and beliefs held uncritically, to a more critical and self-reflective *explicit* theology of faith seeking understanding and intelligent action.[22]

This narration of our lives in relation to God, our theologizing, is passed down to others as shared experiences, stories, forms of worship, creeds and confessions, sacred texts, the lived experience and rituals of community, and a shared framework for making sense of the world. This process is a constant negotiation between what we inherit from sources such as tradition and Scripture and from our own experiences in the world. And we must learn to express our understanding of the Christian faith in a language that is intelligible and credible in that contemporary context.

Theology thus becomes a basis for wrestling with broad claims about reality and the meaning of life, a task that can be aided by resources from wider culture for understanding how to express convictions. Lutheran theologian Ted Peters grapples with this process of theological discernment when he asks, "How can the Christian faith, first experienced and symbolically articulated in an ancient culture now long out-of-date, speak meaningfully to human existence today as we experience it amid a worldview dominated by natural science, secular self-understanding, and the worldwide cry for freedom?"[23]

In this book, our theological reflection is focused on technology, and specifically on the internet and digital technologies, often described as "new media." This kind of reflection exhibits traits of what is called *contextual theology*, a theological endeavor seeking to articulate a practical theology rooted in the experience of the individual or community. Contextual theology offers an explicit dialogue between the past, represented by Scripture and the Christian tradition, and the present, represented particularly by personal and community experience.[24] It pays attention to the experiences of individuals or groups, the mediation of those experiences through culture, and the social location, shaped by factors such as gender, age, ethnicity, socioeconomics, health, and place at the center or margins of power. The last factor is particularly important when considering how social location empowers people to ask theological questions that are new, relevant, and demanding of answers, and also how social location prevents or oppresses theological voices, silencing them or pushing them to the margins.

If, as Kathryn Tanner asserts, Christian theology must be comprehensive because all aspects of the universe are in some form of relationship with God, then theology must grapple with new digital technologies and media. To do that kind of theologizing, Tanner argues, one should not attempt to become an expert in all things but rather draw from the knowledge and wisdom of others who are already steeped in that field.[25] Thus, in this book the authors seek to complement each other's expertise in theology and media, respectively, allowing the conversation between disciplines to develop into theological reflection upon technology and media. Our purpose is to constructively explore the theme of the network in light of the intersection between contemporary media culture and the Christian faith.

While religion and technology are often seen as a fraught or even antagonistic pairing, we argue that theology can and must engage technology and new media to offer a holistic theological response to new media culture. Theologian and bioethicist Ronald Cole-Turner asks,

> Can theology—that communal process by which the church's faith seeks to understand— . . . can theology aim at understanding technology? Can we put the words *God* and *technology* together in any kind of meaningful sentence? Can theology guess what God is doing in today's technology? Or by our silence do we leave it utterly godless? Can we have a theology of technology that comprehends, gives meaning to, dares to influence the direction and set limits to this explosion of new powers?[26]

In addressing these kinds of questions, we acknowledge that all theology is articulated in the language, context, and culture of its day. To describe what we understand to be the shape and content of the gospel, the good news of Jesus Christ, will mean using concepts, ideas, and symbols that make the language intelligible and relevant to those we are communicating with. We also acknowledge, following Lesslie Newbigin, that all culture and language is critiqued by that same gospel.[27]

In a manner similar to the method of correlation proposed by theologian Paul Tillich, we suggest that our culture, including the dimensions connected to digital technologies and media, raises questions about human life and the human condition that the gospel must address.[28] To address these questions and to speak into the networked world in which we are living in a way that clearly communicates the gospel, we must draw upon the riches of the Christian tradition in dialogue with the present, while keeping an eye on the future. Thus, our networked theology seeks to understand the gospel in light of the world in which we live and to faithfully communicate that understanding in both word and deed in this networked world.

The Relationship between the Network and Theology

So how can theology and the metaphor of the network be brought together? According to Stanley Grenz, the theologian is a poet who "crafts meaningful pictures about our world and our relationship to the transcendent."[29] This crafting gives life to images and metaphors drawn from contemporary society that can be used to describe and make tangible people's spiritual beliefs and ideas about God, themselves, and the world around them. In this book we seek to do that crafting in a collaborative exploration that makes theology visible through the eyes of media studies and the network metaphor. By bringing theology into conversation with the idea of the network, a useful conceptualization of networked theology emerges, enabling us to discuss the opportunities and challenges that digital culture presents to Christian communities.

Jesus's parables of the kingdom of God are rooted in this kind of contemporary exploration of his message of good news and our relationships with God and others. In these stories, which were a key component of Jesus's preaching, the kingdom of God expresses the idea of a future vision of well-being and *shalom* under God's rule, as well as the idea of any place and time where God exercises ruling power.[30] When Jesus says, "The time is fulfilled, and the kingdom of God has come near; repent, and believe in the good news" (Mark 1:15), we get a glimpse of both the coming hope of God's rule and peace and the expectation of experiencing that in the present. Using examples from the everyday world of his listeners, Jesus describes the kingdom of God as a small, growing mustard seed, the yeast in bread, a treasure hidden in a field, a pearl of great price, and a net cast into the sea.

In our age of networked media and culture, what would be the equivalent parables of the kingdom? For example, could we tell a parable that begins, "The kingdom of God is like a smartphone with endless battery life and unlimited data" or "The kingdom of God is like a wireless network connecting all kinds of people"? Dwight Friesen, in *Thy Kingdom Connected*, says that the "vision of a networked kingdom" of God is an ideal way to understand how the faith community should behave and interact in our current social reality.[31] Friesen uses the parable of the yeast from the Gospel of Matthew (13:33) as an allegory for how the church should exist as a living, spreadable reality of closely interdependent relationships. He links the idea of active yeast to the concept of the network, which brings together individual nodes into a dynamic system of relational connections. He calls on the church to "shift perceptions from atomized individuals to interconnected relational networks" and so seeks to provide a new map that presents the kingdom of God as a networked kingdom.[32]

In describing how the image of the network can shape theology, Friesen draws on missiologist Paul Hiebert's categories of bounded and centered sets, which have proven influential not only in the areas of mission and evangelism but also in Christian engagement with social justice and spiritual formation.[33] Hiebert's ideas have been used to challenge the idea that entry into the kingdom of God is only a movement across a boundary as a result of a particular event or action, such as praying the sinner's prayer or being baptized. Instead, mission in a networked, relational environment focuses on how people reorient themselves toward God and begin a trajectory of movement toward Christ as the center of their lives. Thus, there is a paradigm shift from encouraging a single-moment event or decision to recognizing a process of alignment with Jesus through relational connections. In Friesen's networked kingdom, Christians are formed and made more Christlike as they continually encounter the living God, not just as a distant, future objective but also in and through the relationships with others—mediated by the Holy Spirit—in which Christ is present.

Seeing the kingdom of God as a network provides a framework for how we interact with God, others, and the world around us. One of the strands of this book looks at Jesus's teaching to love God and love our neighbor and asks who and where our neighbors are in a networked world and how we should act toward them. Tied to this are questions about how to do justice, love mercy, and walk humbly with God in that network culture. The idea of the kingdom as a network also alerts us to the wide range of people and relationships in both church and wider communities (in both physical and online environments) and the possibilities for encountering God in and through them.

The idea of the network highlights not only how we encounter various people and relationships but also the variety of ways in which those relationships are organized. The network can promote flattened rather than hierarchical structures, along with relationships that allow more dynamic interaction rather than being unresponsive and static. This creates sources of creativity and participation that promote connectedness within Christian community, with the "called out" people of God existing together in a system of interdependence and interaction. However, the network can also create tensions and anxiety when it is seen to challenge or undermine aspects of the Christian life, particularly communal life and faith. This book highlights both of these dimensions—the opportunities and challenges—brought about by new forms of communication, new proposals for community, new kinds of interaction, and issues of accountability and ethics in the networked world. In doing so, it seeks to assist individual Christians and church communities as they negotiate the opportunities and challenges of network culture.

At one level, networked theology is about theology and media in dialogue, as it seeks to make connections and generate relationships between the two areas that can lead to fruitful and insightful conversation. For theology to grapple with and speak into the church as a network, it needs to interact more fully with the expertise available in media and communication disciplines. Similarly, media and communication disciplines can learn how religion, technology, and media interact within a faith community by engaging with theology, which informs about the core concepts, practices, and experiences that shape that community.

At a deeper level, this book seeks to engage Christians in their faithful living in a networked world, encompassing not only their individual spiritual lives and the lives of their communities but also their living wisely and well within the wider world. It explores the complexities of the relationships between Christian life and media culture in order to aid the church in thinking critically and constructively about those relationships so as to live out the good news of Jesus Christ in our contemporary world. At this level, networked theology is about seeking to love God and love neighbor with all our hearts, minds, and bodies in a way that helps us to live well in a media culture and also to shape that culture for the sake of the gospel of Christ.

A Guide to *Networked Theology*

Networked Theology explores core issues and trends that influence Christian beliefs and practices in a world increasingly dependent on and wrapped in new media. *Networked Theology* thus highlights and analyzes how religion is practiced both online and offline in our information-based society and shows that digital practices and innovations in religion online often point toward larger cultural shifts in how faith is perceived and shaped offline.

We argue that serious theological discourse is important in order to fully understand how new media shape our everyday lives and the ethical impact of our technological engagement on our perception of what it means to be human. A central goal of this book is to bring new media studies and theory into conversation with theology in a new way. We, the authors of this book, have unique backgrounds making us well suited for such a task.

Heidi A. Campbell is a media studies scholar, specializing in digital culture and new media theory, who also has training in theology. Since the mid-1990s she has been studying the relationship between religion and the internet, with a focus on how Christian communities have used and responded to the internet. She completed one of the first PhDs in the world on religion and the internet, combining the study of computer-mediated communication with practical theology to investigate the impact religious communities online might have on people's perception of and involvement in the church and in Christian communities offline. Over the past two decades her work has explored questions of religious community, identity, and authority online, as well as religious communities' negotiations with digital media. As director of the Network for New Media, Religion, and Digital Culture Studies, she strives to build bridges between academic disciplines, such as theology and media studies, to create a vibrant interdisciplinary conversation about the extent to which new media technologies are affecting religious communities' authority, identity, and rituals in a globalized society. Through this book she desires to bring her expertise on the social and ethical implications of digital culture into dialogue with her training and personal study in the theology of technology to help the church think more critically about how technology can and should intersect with faith in the network society.

Stephen Garner is a theologian with expertise in systematic, public, and contextual theology as well as a background in computer science. Prior to his theological studies, he completed postgraduate studies in software engineering, conducted research in the application of machine learning systems to real-world databases, and worked in the information technology industry as a programmer analyst. In his theological teaching and research, he has maintained an interest in technology and media from the theological perspective, with his PhD research examining Christian theological responses to new digital technologies, such as artificial intelligence, virtual reality, and the ideology of transhumanism. He has also served on the New Zealand Interchurch Bioethics Council and continues to research in the areas of religion and transhumanism, public and contextual theology, religion and popular culture, and theology and technology. He believes that theology must engage with the everyday communities we find ourselves in, seeking to offer something distinctly Bible-based to the church and world.

This collaborative book offers insights into our shared conversation, demonstrating what each field of study has to offer in creating a theologically informed response to new media culture. We assert that the effort to understand the impact of new media and the network society on Christianity requires a more in-depth and multidisciplinary conversation than is currently taking place within Christian scholarship. To date, much of the scholarly work on the intersection of new digital media and theology has taken one of two forms: either guides for Christians on how media should be used for purposes such as evangelism or worship, or appraisals of new media often grounded in overly pessimistic or overly optimistic assumptions about the nature of new media and their potential religious and cultural impact. We suggest a need for reflection that does more than offer advice about how churches should or should not engage with media and instead interrogates how the use of new media correlates with social and religious values. In an age of new media, we must pay attention to the theological and ethical impact of technology. This requires a nuanced understanding of both media theory, to help explain the function and revolutionary nature of new media, and the theology of technology, which provides resources for constructing a faith-based response to digital culture.

This book synthesizes key findings from our previous and current work in digital media studies, theology of technology, and sociology of religion and technology on the relationship between the Christian faith, new media, and digital culture. Thus, it is theoretically grounded and practical. We draw on scholarly research on the concepts of religious community, identity, and authority in relation to the internet, as well as on case studies of Christian engagement with the internet, to explore what a theology of media could look like in an age of new media. We also provide theological reflections on the effect of digital space, mobility, information authenticity, and technologized presence on traditional theological notions of truth, being, community, and authority.

Chapter 1 offers an introduction to the theology of technology, providing some definitions of technology and bridging from those definitions to more specific media technologies. It then traces a path through the history of the Christian church, examining how Christian communities have negotiated new technologies and media. This leads to three key responses to technology within the Christian church—optimism, pessimism, and instrumentalism—each of which highlights a particular dimension of technological negotiation. Finally, the chapter introduces the idea of appropriate technology, enabling us to live wisely in our networked world. Thus, it offers an overview of theological tools and frameworks that help us look at the relationship between media technology and theology.

This leads us to chapter 2, which offers a crash course in new media theory. It outlines the difference between old or traditional mass media and new media by highlighting key characteristics of this new generation of digital, computer-networked technologies. It also discusses what is really "new" about new media, not just in terms of technological features, but in terms of the culture that new media facilitate and the social practices and expectations they create. The chapter introduces key concepts such as the myth of interactivity, media convergence, and the rhetoric surrounding the transition from Web 1.0 to Web 3.0. It then highlights conditions of the network society that create a distinct set of expectations of how the world does and should function. Issues discussed include patterns related to constant contact, publicized privacy, remix culture, and networked individualism, all of which have important theological implications.

Chapter 3 addresses the potential impact of technological embeddedness on our values and behaviors as our daily lives become increasingly mediated by digital and mobile technologies. It considers how digital media promote and encourage certain social practices and religious understandings. This is done by presenting the concept of networked religion, which encapsulates some of the important trends in practicing religion online and highlights dominant traits related to religious community, identity, authority, practice, and authenticity. This discussion provides synthesis of twenty years of research on how religion is practiced and perceived online and what implications this has for the Christian tradition. It demonstrates that key characteristics of online religion are mirrored in contemporary offline religious culture. These changes in religious practice often have not been recognized by Christian groups and churches and are in need of careful consideration.

Chapter 4 explores how our technological and media environment engages with and shapes particular areas of our theology. Using the motif of Jesus's command to love our neighbor, this chapter asks who is a neighbor in our networked world, where are they located, and how we ought to treat them.

It examines particular aspects of Christian theology, such as physical presence, community, identity, and agency, about which new media raise significant challenges and opportunities. We end this chapter with the challenge to find avenues for developing theologically based, appropriate technology that stands in continuity with Christianity's past, present, and future.

In chapter 5 we map out a framework for how religious communities and groups can develop their own "theology of new media." A four-stage strategy, adapted from the religious-social shaping approach to technology, is translated into a set of questions and areas of reflection that Christian groups can use to consider how their media use does or should relate to their community's beliefs and mission. This provides a practical framework for developing a theologically informed media strategy for communities or even families. It enables Christians to actively reflect on their technology use in light of their faith and consider how new media technologies themselves, or their patterns of use, may need to be adapted to be in line with their core values and convictions.

Finally, chapter 6 offers a proposal for what a robust, theologically informed, appropriate technology might look like and how it might speak to both the church and the wider public. We ask in particular: How can technology and media address some of our previous questions about neighbors and neighborhood? To answer this, we take the text from Micah 6:8 to do justice, love mercy, and walk humbly with God as a framework for identifying aspects of appropriate technology that maintain a love of neighbor, an engagement with the wider world, and a focus on using technology and media as a form of worship of God.

theology of technology 101

Understanding the Relationship between Theology and Technology

We begin our exploration of networked theology by exploring the historical and contemporary dialogue between technology and theology within the context of the Christian church. We argue that if technology and new media are the environments in which we find ourselves, it is important to consider how we might faithfully engage with these areas and the ways they are shaping us. Theology of technology is an area of study that has sought to offer theological reflection on the history and development of technology. This chapter unpacks the relationship between technology and the Christian church in order to provide a theological context to discuss how the emergence of digital technologies can and should draw on a long tradition of ethical reflection. We begin this introduction to a theology of technology by looking at how technology has been defined, some different ways the church has negotiated with technology and media, and common Christian responses to technology. This, in turn, will lead to further discussion in later chapters as to what is an appropriate response to technology and media in network society, where we are increasingly wrapped in media.

Defining Technology

Searching for a single, concise definition of technology can prove problematic. Etymologically the term originates in the Indo-European stem *tekhn-*, which is connected to woodworking and seen in the Greek term *technē*, meaning "art," "craft," or "skill." The latter goes beyond working with material things and includes manipulating concepts and language, such as forms of writing and speaking (like rhetoric) or particular intellectual disciplines or ways of thinking. In Latin, *texere* related first to weaving and later to construction or fabrication. By the eighteenth century the term had begun to narrow in definition; it excluded the broad range of artistic endeavors and instead focused on the application of science, particularly with respect to practical mechanics.[1]

This shift to focusing on mechanisms and mechanics has led to a common definition of technology as tools or machines. As David Hopper puts it, technology is concerned with the human community creating and inventing assorted tools, machines, and mechanisms to manipulate and exploit the natural world. Furthermore, technological application influences not only creation but also the human community, shaping the rhythms of everyday life.[2] Such a definition of technology is consistent with the familiar understanding, which David Pullinger expresses, "that society develops the technology it needs and then uses it to produce goods and services for the creation of wealth and for human culture to flourish. Needs and wishes come first, and then technology simply fulfils them."[3] Thus, we need shelter, so we develop forms of clothing and housing; we need stable food sources, so we develop agriculture; and we desire to communicate over a longer distance than we can shout, so we develop semaphore, the telegraph, and radio. This way of looking at technology is linked with the augmentation of human abilities such as mobility, communication, and thinking.

This predominant view of technology as mechanism, mechanics, and applied practical knowledge reduces technology primarily to an instrument, seeing it simply as a tool to accomplish specific tasks. This parallels the way that media have typically been viewed. Peter Horsfield notes that this approach to media as tools or instruments started in the 1920s with the development of mass media, which aimed to address large, broad audiences through cinema, radio, and newspapers. Attempts to understand the power of media and how they shaped society led to ways of looking at media so that they (and their effects) might be measured in linear, cause-and-effect models.[4] More recently, though, both technology and media have been seen to possess more than just an instrumental nature. Media technology is understood to include epistemological and sociological dimensions, which combine with the instrumental to create a view of technology that is complex and dynamic.

Looking at technology primarily as a tool to achieve some human goal, typically by transcending the natural abilities of human beings, is one of three interwoven perspectives that Susan White identifies in her examination of the interplay between technology and Christian worship.[5] First, technology can be seen as artifacts produced by manufacturing processes, whether a computer, pen, fire, chemical compound, or software system. This is perhaps the most common way of thinking about technology. The second view sees technology as describing not so much the manufactured artifacts as the processes and structures needed to produce these things. Various kinds of human skills and techniques combine with the manufacturing infrastructure to comprise technology. The third way to look at technology is to see it as the cultural structures that provide the inclination and motivation to support the technological systems—becoming a pervasive "technoculture." White argues that these three views interpenetrate each other to create a vision of technology as a "sociotechnical system in which hardware, technique, and a particular ideological frame of reference combine to aid in the pursuit of essentially pragmatic ends, generally associated with the augmentation of human capabilities."[6]

This approach implies that technology is inherently connected to and embedded within human culture and values, with a particular emphasis on the achievement of pragmatic ends. Similar views to this are reflected in Ian Barbour's definition of technology as "the application of organized knowledge to practical tasks by ordered systems of people and machines"[7] and Rudi Volti's opinion that technology is "a system based on the application of knowledge, manifested in physical objects and organizational forms, for the attainment of specific goals."[8] However, while emphasis is often placed on practical, purposeful definitions of technology, such definitions are not exclusive. For example, technologist Kevin Kelly argues that while technology might start with the experience of the human condition and also with scientific method, it exists to allow human beings to pursue novelty and experience.[9] Thus, technology becomes a way of understanding ourselves and the world and bringing something new into existence simply because it can and might be done, even as a spiritual exercise.

Similarly, the instrumental approach has tended to dominate definitions of media. As noted previously, this view of media as instruments or tools dates back to the rise of interest in mass media in the 1920s, when newspapers, film, and radio were engaging large audiences.[10] Questions around how this affected populations, say, with respect to political or commercial interests, led to a desire to see media as something that could be controlled and targeted. Thus, media, and particularly mass media, were reduced to simple and mechanical communication processes or channels that functioned in predictable ways.

This limited way of understanding media was challenged toward the end of the twentieth century as questions were asked of media that the instrumental models could not fully answer. For example, what is the relationship between violence in media and violence in society? What other forms of mediated communication outside of mass media have societies used? And do media really possess a value-neutral character? The outcome of this line of questioning is that media may be seen not only as processes or tools but also in terms of how an entire society or culture exists in a space of constant mediation of information, ideas, behaviors, and values through a variety of media. According to Horsfield, this contextual view, with its attention to cultural processes, understands media "not as instruments carrying a fixed message but as sites where construction, negotiation, and reconstruction of cultural meaning takes place in an ongoing process of maintenance and change of cultural structures, relationships, meanings, and values."[11]

Both the instrumental and cultural approaches to media benefit when they are used together. The instrumental approach is useful in posing questions about the effects of communicating a message, while the cultural approach shapes questions about the societal environment that the process is located within. As with technology, media are simultaneously tools and environments.

Bridging between Technology and Media Technologies

White's and Horsfield's definitions above alert us to the fact that technology and media are multifaceted entities involving, as Stephen Monsma notes, anthropological, sociological, and epistemological dimensions.[12] For example, an anthropological approach might ask if certain facets of a technology can be seen as inherent parts, and thus defining marks, of human beings, individually and communally. Here human beings are first and foremost *homo faber*, makers or creators in their very nature. Sociologically, we might go beyond the concepts of technology and media as manufactured items, a human attribute, or a distinct body of knowledge to see technology as an all-encompassing force within modern society. We might also consider technology as a special form of knowledge, useful to those who want to investigate how knowledge is transferred within or between communities, or to compare different bodies of knowledge (such as methodologies) present in different communities.

Monsma picks up these three dimensions in his theological perspective on technology, where he sees technology as a key human cultural activity, born from human beings as culture creators.[13] Human beings create "integrated patterns of human behavior," and technology is integrated into a web of relationships that permeate human existence, including religious beliefs, customs, and institutions. As we shall see later in this chapter, one example of this is the written word or book, which moves beyond just being a technological artifact into shaping religious and cultural life in various historical contexts. On the other hand, limiting technology merely to one of many human cultural activities can obscure the role of technology in vertical relationships—that is, relationships between humanity and the divine. Technological activity might in fact be seen as a response to God's call. Not only that, but by asserting that technology is the defining mark of humanity, other human distinctives may be obscured. For Monsma, "God calls his children as his image bearers to be formers of culture. As such we purposefully take what is given in God's creation and creatively form it into art, language, laws, social mores, societal institutions—and technological tools and products."[14]

Bringing all these strands together provides us with a definition of technology, and in particular media technology, which we will focus on in this book. Technology is, first and foremost, *a human activity that is carried out within the context provided by God for human beings to exercise their creativity and agency*. This definition possesses both the aspects of pragmatism, seen in problem solving and transforming the natural world, and the aspects of novelty and a human creative trajectory. It recognizes that technology has a significant sociocultural dimension—it is *human* technology—that wraps it in a network of relationships, values, and histories and makes technology dynamic, shaped by and shaping the various feedback loops that exist within that network. Technology includes the artifacts that are produced and the special knowledge and processes that produce those artifacts, as well as the people, practices, and values in a particular time and place. Technology in this way is the environment in which we live.

What this means for how we think about technology and media is that we cannot simply reflect theologically upon the most visible artifacts in the wider technology system. Rather, we must be concerned with the human elements, such as what human activities are served or prevented, what values are implicitly or explicitly present, how technology functions as part of the context of human existence, and the history of communities' negotiation with human creativity, which has a strong pragmatic direction. With this in mind, we now turn to look at how Christianity has negotiated the place of technology in human history.

Historical Negotiation with Technology

Christianity is one of the three major world religions, along with Judaism and Islam, whose adherents are sometimes called the People of the Book. For the

Christian church, identity and faith are shaped by interaction with the Christian Bible, which is composed of the Hebrew Scriptures and the later Christian writings known as the New or Second Testament. The Bible itself can be seen as a tangible expression of technology and media in that it is typically a human-created physical artifact (though other mediated representations are possible) that has been produced by special knowledge. The Bible's form and content, as well as the form and shape of the Christian community, are influenced by distinct social and cultural environments.

While people may not consider Christianity and technology deeply connected in their everyday world, the Bible provides a useful example of how Christianity has been negotiating with technology and media throughout its history. This negotiation is interwoven with disputes over how technology and media should or should not interact with the faith and the ways that technology and media development in wider society have shaped Christianity. This constant negotiation is important to recognize because the way Christianity and other faiths respond to new technologies and media is often predicated on how they responded to technologies and media in the past. In the following section we will discuss specific negotiations with technology—from the oral and written media traditions to contemporary media—through the history of Christianity.

From Oral Traditions to Books and Codices

The early Christian church negotiated between the oral tradition of the day and the written literate traditions also present in that society. Jesus of Nazareth was a skilled and effective orator who, in the Gospels, displays a rabbinic model of teaching based on oral storytelling, discussion, and debate. He identified himself with the poor and the oppressed and used oral forms such as parables to communicate with them, yet he drew on a comprehensive knowledge and interpretation of Jewish sacred written texts. By utilizing oral and written traditions, Jesus gathered around himself a community of disciples who continued in versions of that oral tradition as witnesses to him and bearers of his teaching.[15]

This model of itinerant preaching formed one of the communication strands of the early church. Over time, though, another communicative role developed in the church, that of literate teachers who brought text-based approaches from both Jewish and Greek practices of oral interpretation of written texts. Thus, we find in the Christian writings of the New Testament stylistic practices involving both reflection upon Jewish writings and allusions to Greco-Roman philosophers and poets (e.g., Acts 17:28). Often the two roles were combined, as in the case of people who took letters to a community and then "performed" them for that audience. However, as Horsfield observes, over time the significance of codifying particular accounts of Jesus's life into standardized forms, as well as the connection between literacy and leadership in the church, led to the written text, and particularly the Bible, becoming a source of power and authority.[16]

The adoption of the papyrus codex, a precursor of the book, marked the acceptance of a particular expression of media technology that became a significant part of Christian identity and the Christian church. Moreover, the physical form of the codex, seen as containing the sacred writings and accounts of the faith, became so significant that its protection and veneration were causes of martyrdom. Tension arose between those who gave up the texts under persecution and those who protected them unto death. As Horsfield and Asamoah-Gyadu note, "Stories such as this reinforced the importance and emotional attachment to the codex as an important identity marker for Christianity as a religion of the book rather than just the text. The codex set Christianity apart culturally from groups such as other imperial religions and the literati, who did not adopt the codex for literary purposes until several centuries later."[17]

By the end of the third century, the presence of the written text was well established, particularly after the recognition of Christianity as a state religion in the Roman Empire. This helped stabilize what was being said about Jesus and his followers. Those who were literate stood a better chance at leadership in the church, as the focus on texts favored literate men and created stronger ecclesiastical control by ruling bishops. This also contributed to the marginalization of women in the church from their initial position of supporters, patrons, and coworkers, as authority shifted to a church administration influenced by Roman societal structures. Moreover, it was possible to name some texts as heterodox, if not heretical, and control their impact. The Bible shifted from being a book that was read for its content to being an artifact to be decorated and venerated in its own right.[18] In addition to the Hebrew Scriptures, Christian accounts of Jesus of Nazareth and his followers and helpful letters to churches were collected together and declared the sacred Word of God.

Thus, a form of technology found in the codex and the book made its way into the Christian church and shaped the faith itself. In particular, the book as a technology influenced ways of thinking about the sources of authority in the church, which were based on who could read and write. The book as a technology created control of access to and use of the Bible and thus the authority of the collected and authorized (or canonical) writings of the church, as the Bible became encoded in a static form. Authority then rested with the interpreters of that static form rather than in direct engagement with the biblical text. Moreover, the book emphasized that the technology of writing was something that could convey power and organization across cultures and geographies.

Horsfield and Paul Teusner develop this idea further when they argue that one can only understand how Christianity negotiated media—and we would add technology—by observing the relationship between religion and media in the overall matrix of cultural life.[19] For them, no aspect of Christianity is unmediated, because every experience and concept of the faith is caught up in the network of relationships found in the language used to describe them, human experience, the politics of church and society, relationships—including power relationships—and historical-cultural contexts. The Bible is a product of these things, and its usage and role are shaped by their particularities.

Literacy as Power

With the decline of the Roman Empire came a corresponding decline in literacy, with the emphasis upon the written text limited to the imperial Roman church. This was manifest particularly in monasteries, which served as libraries and production houses for books. Monasteries became the centers of writing and education, as well as the preservation of language, especially Latin. The preservation of literacy brought with it political and cultural power through the development of law codes and libraries, centers where legal documents, records, and charters were stored and copied. It also meant that the Christian tradition was further codified in terms of liturgy and doctrine, as spoken, sung, and enacted forms of worship were recorded in a fixed structure, enabling an illiterate society to faithfully replicate these practices. Horsfield summarizes: "Through the control of language and literacy, the male clergy celibate class came to exercise control over all aspects of Christian life. This linguistic power would not be challenged until the time of printing, when vernacular languages regained political power."[20]

The enhancement of printing technology during the Renaissance had significant religious implications, again highlighting the complex interaction between culture, technology, and society. The availability and influence of printing technology grew in the mid-1400s with the development of the Gutenberg printing press using cast metallic type, the establishment of a paper-making industry, mass distribution transport networks, and the European Renaissance environment. The resulting reproduction of old manuscripts (such as in classical philosophy and mathematics), an increased desire for literacy, developments in natural philosophy and science, and social and political developments all contributed to the renegotiation of media and technology. Examples of this can be seen in the way current events were recorded and disseminated, the production of printed maps, printed text becoming a primary form of social communication, more rapid transmission of ideas (including religious ideas), and increased literacy among the public.[21]

Francis Bacon (1561–1626) is a good example of someone from this time who influenced the social and cultural negotiation of media and technology. Bacon's empiricism, the idea that knowledge comes from sensory observation of the world, led not only to a modern scientific approach that connects hypothesis to observation to theory to understanding but also to a narrative of purpose that saw the relationship between science and technology develop. Bacon argued that human beings were to shape the natural world in such a way as to bring about a better world for humanity—a return to the Garden of Eden—because human beings have the power to observe what needs to be corrected in the world and the divine mandate to make those corrections through human agency.[22]

John Briggs notes the close association argued for by Bacon between the philosophical study of nature—leading to sciences such as physics—and religion. These new sciences worked together with God's purposes, Bacon thought, to save humanity both materially (e.g., from illness and suffering) and spiritually (e.g., undoing humanity's separation from God). Natural philosophy, with its application of human reason, was seen as the handmaiden of traditional religion, a powerful subordinate seeking to restore humankind's dominion over a rebellious nature. With the ultimate goal of a return to Eden, to original perfection, science and technology are to serve humanity by alleviating human suffering. Thus, while God and faith in God work to repair the human soul, humanity can work to repair creation.[23] In this way Bacon firmly connects technological progress, seen in natural philosophy, with divine purpose. In *Novum Organum* he writes, "Only let the human race recover that right over nature which belongs to it by divine bequest, and let power be given to it; the exercise thereof will be governed by sound reason and true religion."[24]

Mitcham and Grote note that the theological virtue of charity—using technology to help people—has been the virtue most often used to provide the strongest case for technology. Bacon's influence developed a strand of thought that asserted that the technological endeavor was purposed to the relief of suffering, motivated by charity.[25]

Printing and the Wider World of Text

The development of printing allowed for larger-scale publishing and distribution of religious and other books. Different parts of the church responded differently to the rise of printed religious text. To increase reading of the Scriptures among common people, William Tyndale in the sixteenth century worked to produce Bibles in the local vernacular, in this case English, while his contemporary Martin Luther produced similar translations in German.

The printing press facilitated the spread of religious ideas and propaganda, including Luther's Ninety-Five Theses (1517) and John Calvin's *Institutes of the Christian Religion* (1536). Such works were disseminated to a wider audience by the ability to produce and copy texts with increasing ease. Protestant and Roman Catholic churches sought to use printing for their own purposes and maintained close control over it (e.g., the Roman Catholic Church produced the *Index Librorum Prohibitorum*, or List of Prohibited Books). Horsfield notes that the Roman Catholic Church had an early investment in the use of printing, a good example of which is Ignatius of Loyola's *Spiritual Exercises*, which embodied a structured system of spiritual formation formally approved by Pope Paul III in 1548, and which was, and still is, widely read. However, not everyone in the church saw printing as a good thing. Many people had concern about printed media, including the fact that printed text lost the aesthetic of the written manuscript produced by expert calligraphers and illuminators. Furthermore, the mechanism of printing removed the act of human contemplation on the text from the process of copying and writing, where the scribe is initiated into the divine mysteries being recorded through the process of creating the written text.[26]

Changes brought about by printing were significant. Printing not only changed the way information and ideas spread but also elevated text so that it became the dominant medium of communication both formally and socially. Printing allowed bureaucracies to develop through the social and institutional standardization brought about by using text. For Christianity, printing had many implications, including the development of a movement accepting Enlightenment rationalism over spiritual knowledge of God. It also led to the establishment of denominations such as Presbyterianism and Methodism. The failure of any one particular Christian group to completely dominate its context led to groups of Christians forming their own distinctive communities. Such groups were supported by access to printed Bibles in the vernacular and the production of printed material to educate and attract new members and defend against other groups. Horsfield contends, "If we think of media culturally rather than instrumentally, it can be argued that different media prefer particular forms or structures of religious faith to others. From this perspective, I'd argue that the denominational structure of Christianity that emerged during the Modern period, emerged because it was the structure of Christianity most appropriate for cultures structured by printing."[27] He argues that print technology led to increased individual use and interpretation of the Bible. Worship materials became standardized in hymn and prayer books, demanding increased literacy among clergy and laity, and theological studies became predominantly a book-based, academic discipline.

This kind of splintering produced by the development and application of various media technologies available through printing was mirrored in the later development of electronic media such as television and the internet. For example, Stewart Hoover notes that the development of cable and satellite television in the United States in the 1970s made it possible for religion to be broadcast to niche audiences (e.g., Christian evangelicalism), with particular emphases on theological and cultural distinctives.[28] No longer limited to set time slots on network television or radio, smaller groups could become broadcasters, adopting radio and television to produce relatively cheap electronic media to be consumed by a target audience or, in the case of religious marketing and evangelism, develop new target audiences.

As with previous negotiations between religion and technology, the adoption of electronic media technology is not uniform, with some rejecting it, others embracing it, and still others vacillating between these responses. Hoover notes, however, that "most people seem to want to say that they will regularly accept, reject, and contest media in ways that are relevant to their values and their beliefs."[29] It is to these responses to technology and media that we now turn.

Responses to Technology and Media

Christian responses to technology and media reflect a somewhat ambiguous state of affairs, with some seeing technology and media in very positive ways, while others are quite pessimistic about them. Within the range of responses to technology, several trends can be seen. Science and religion scholar Ian Barbour offers a helpful threefold typology that sums up the most common responses to technology. Barbour's work is influenced by the work of twentieth-century theologian H. Richard Niebuhr, who outlined various ways in which the relationship between Christianity and culture can be understood.[30] Barbour's own scheme employs three categories of individuals: those optimistic about technology, those pessimistic about it, and those who view technology as an ambiguous instrument of power.[31] Although any scheme like this tends to reduce the complexity and ambiguity of its subject to something simpler than its reality, Barbour's categories provide a helpful starting point for thinking about how different parts of the Christian community conceive of and engage with technology.

Technological Optimism

One response to technology and media is to see them as a liberating force that brings an overall improvement to the human condition. From this perspective, technology ushers in labor-saving devices and access to information and entertainment, and it improves productivity, leading to economic growth. Technological optimism sees media and technology as making the world a better place for humanity, increasing people's choice of available products and services. People also gain social and geographic mobility and control over nature and the human body, such as through birth control and reproductive technologies. In this case, Christians might see the endowment of human beings with intellectual and technological prowess as a way in which human technological activity is divinely "baptized," provided by God to improve life and, in some cases, to establish the kingdom of God here on earth. In this pragmatic view, technology and knowledge do not exist for their own sake but are to be channeled to provide "material mercies" for humankind.[32]

In response to the internet and new media, technological optimism highlights the positive ways those technologies might be used in mission and evangelism as well as church worship. Christ's commandment in the Gospel of Matthew (28:18–20) to go and make disciples of all nations becomes a mandate to use whatever media are available to achieve that task, be it print, radio, television, or the internet. The promise of access to communities who have not yet heard the gospel sits well with the vision of being witnesses of Christ to "the ends of the earth" portrayed in the book of Acts (1:7–8).

Technological optimism sees technology and media as having a positive impact on the nature and function of the church. Engagement with the internet and new media becomes a way for churches to promote themselves and their causes to a wider public. They can not only spread their teaching but also attract new members and engage younger generations. Technology allows members to access church services at different times through podcasts and video feeds, and it helps maintain regular and extensive pastoral support networks. As such, technology serves to maintain church structures; we shall see it can also challenge them. Finally, with a plethora of church management software now available, technology and the internet can be used to manage the daily running of churches.

However, this optimistic view can mask a variety of problems inherent in technology. For example, Barbour notes that when technology is looked at through an overly optimistic lens, things like environmental problems and human risks associated with technology are often minimized or seen as problems that can be solved through the application of another technology. Moreover, the interaction between economic, political, and social institutions and technology is downplayed, because technology is seen as a value-neutral instrument. Questions about who can afford and access technology, the disproportionate consumption of resources in the industrialized world, and the nature of power relationships between technology, corporations, politicians, civil servants, and various publics are either minimized or considered not to be in the interests of the community. Graham Houston argues that the increasing control of the technological world by a decreasing number of experts and technocrats is challenging the presuppositions that technology is a democratic medium; technology may be easy to use, but users only get the world that others want them to have.[33]

Technological Pessimism

Whereas the previous response promotes unbridled optimism about technology and its effects on humanity, technological pessimism takes an opposite trajectory. For some, the way technology pervades modern society results in a number of negative effects. Technological pessimism highlights the suppression of individuality and creativity within society because of the quest for technological efficiency through mass production. It also highlights the influence of mass media as dehumanizing people and relationships through impersonal communication structures.

These perceived effects are typically coupled with the fear, often couched in sociological terms, that technology has become an autonomous, all-powerful system that most people have little or no understanding of or control over and that reduces the choices an individual can make. Barbour notes that "some critics assert that technology is not just a set of adaptable tools for human use but an all-encompassing form of life, a pervasive structure with its own logic and dynamic."[34] Pullinger observes that technological development, with its related scientific exploration, tends to happen outside the public eye, leading to new developments suddenly appearing "fully grown" in the world, such as developments in genetics or biotechnology or even the internet, which had existed in some form for decades before the public became aware of it. Furthermore, these new developments often appear to be imposed on society by some external, alien force, causing people either to adapt to technology or to be left on the margins of society. This force, sometimes referred to as technological determinism, removes the element of volition from technological use, or at least reduces it to a choice about which form of the technology to adopt.[35] For example, you might be offered the choice of different computers or operating systems to do your work or access a public system such as a government department. However, the option of living or working a different way is not permitted, a fact that is often wrapped up in a myth of progress.

One of the most well-known advocates of technological pessimism was the French theologian and philosopher Jacques Ellul. Ellul described technology, or more specifically "*technique*," as "the totality of methods rationally arrived at and having absolute efficiency (for a given stage of development) in every field of human activity."[36] In this view of technology, a quest for efficiency through the application of human reason and logic ultimately dehumanizes individuals and communities by reducing them to impersonal, economic units. Here technological culture becomes the milieu in which human beings now live. This is an environment determined not by nature but by the complex interdependencies between artificial components of an all-embracing technological ecosystem that seeks efficiency. In this environment humanity must adapt to technological culture or be marginalized, because technology seeks to integrate all things, people, ideologies, and institutions into a unified worldview that pushes the values of technology over its creators.

Ellul saw technology as bringing some benefits to humankind, but for him every "beneficial" technological development included unforeseen negative implications that outweighed the benefits. Within the world of the internet and new media, this pessimism is seen in framing the internet as magnifying problems and flaws present within humanity and its social structures. The internet is perceived as leading to the breakdown of face-to-face relationships, replacing the physical worship community, and encouraging mediated interaction even within religious and spiritual life.[37] Additionally, some see it as providing access to naive and potentially dangerous and heterodox religious ideas and teachings leading people away from orthodox faith in Christ.[38] The argument here is that although access to information, other cultures, and freedom of speech is a good thing, believers may not have the capacity to critically evaluate all the competing ideas and values made available by digital media and communications and be drawn away from authentic expressions of the faith. Moreover, the Vatican's Pontifical Council for Social Communications expresses concern that the internet provides a pathway for the young into "consumerism, pornographic and violent fantasy, and pathological isolation,"[39] a concern echoed in other parts of the wider church.[40]

The pessimistic response is powerful, often highlighting very real human issues brought about by the presence, development, and application of technology. However, technology is multifaceted, and what might be one person's peril is another person's benefit. Barbour argues that the recognition of the social context of technology is significant, but he also points to how social, political, and economic forces operate upon the very technology shaping those forces.[41] Ronald Cole-Turner cites the example that while technologically supported market forces were promoting genetically modified foods in the United Kingdom in the 1990s, consumers exerted their own influence through consumer choice to reject the particular technology at that time.[42] Moreover, Barbour contends, pessimism may become self-fulfilling when resistance to technological development is seen as futile, muting the desire to change the system and effectively relinquishing power to those technological systems. Instead, Barbour asks that we locate alternative values that will challenge and shape the values of the individuals, institutions, and communities involved in technological development and application. If alternative values can be articulated, questioning technological dependence and the material progress that gives rise to narratives of oppression, and if humans develop better relationships with each other and with nature, then maybe technological endeavor can be reshaped in better, more positive directions.

Technological Ambiguity

Sitting between technological optimism and pessimism is the category of individuals who approach technology as an ambiguous instrument of power. What is most important here is the social context of technology, considering how its development, application, and consequences determine its moral value. For example, a hammer might be considered a positive tool in the hands of a person building a house, but it may become a negative, destructive tool used to destroy that same house. The key for proponents of this approach lies in the intentions of those using the tool and the consequences of its use. What is the intention of the hammer wielder? What are the consequences of its being wielded? And what framework of values do we use to evaluate both intention and consequences? For example, the "builder" might be part of a development process that is harming the environment, and the "destroyer" might be part of a much-needed restoration project. Tools, like the hammer in this example, can function simultaneously in positive and negative ways.

This is clearly illustrated through a recent television commercial advertising an internet banking service. In the commercial a man walks into a bank. A little while later he leaves in a distressed state, on the verge of tears. The cause of his anguish is the fact that he has just signed up for the bank's internet banking service and will never need to come to the bank again. On the one hand, the customer now has access to a range of online banking services that the bank claims will make his life better. On the other hand, the human relationships the customer has developed at his local bank are now in jeopardy. The television commercial ends with the customer standing outside the bank, face pressed against the glass, longingly looking inside and stating he's not sure if he's ready for the future.

Alongside concerns about technology is a corresponding sense of wonder and awe at the power and scope of human technological agency. The customer in the commercial is excited that he can do his banking online, twenty-four hours a day, and that the technology will allow him to use his time differently, and hopefully more productively, in the future. Thus, the technology in question is perceived as an ambiguous instrument of power—simultaneously imbuing it with power and limiting it.

This ambiguous stance echoes the response of those like Barbour, for whom technology is not value-neutral in that it is neither wholly, inherently good nor wholly, inherently evil. Technology does not occur in a vacuum; technologies are social constructions created in response to guiding values present in society and its institutions. This view reflects the cultural dimension of technology (which Susan White alerted us to earlier), where ideologies and pragmatism combine to shape technology in part through political and commercial processes. However, Barbour comments that the public ability or desire to engage with these types of processes may, in many cases, be thwarted by those in power or muted in the face of the enormity of the task.[43]

A good example of this perception is the Pontifical Council for Social Communications' response to the internet highlighting what it sees as its ambiguous nature: "Although the virtual reality of cyberspace cannot substitute for real interpersonal community, the incarnational reality of the sacraments and the liturgy, or the immediate and direct proclamation of the gospel, it can complement them, attract people to a fuller experience of the life of faith, and enrich the religious lives of users."[44] Here technology and media are seen to possess both positive and negative dimensions. They can build people up, particularly in the religious or spiritual sense, and they can also divert people from an ideal of what true spirituality and human life should look like. For Barbour, it is this ambiguous response to technology that most closely fits within what he calls a biblical outlook, which recognizes that human relationships with technology can become idolatrous and displace God, especially when technology is used as an unjust instrument of power over human beings and the natural world. However, technology can also become the medium through which human beings respond to God in creative, compassionate, and just ways. "The biblical understanding of human nature," Barbour says, "is realistic about the abuses of power and the institutionalization of self-interest. But it also is idealistic in its demands for social justice in the distribution of the fruits of technology. It brings together celebration of human creativity and suspicion of human power."[45]

This bifocal view of technology, which simultaneously celebrates and suspects it, makes the response to technology both simple and incredibly complex. As Cole-Turner points out, our technology, "for all its good, is constantly on the edge of sin, exploitation, and greed. It is, after all, *human technology*, beset by our weaknesses."[46] Not only that, but the very ambiguity of our response to technology and media might suggest that we no longer recognize technology or media when we see them. As Monsma puts it, "Technology and its results are so much with us that, like the air we breathe, their presence and effects go unnoticed and unanalyzed. As a result, modern technology and all it entails are often accepted by default, with few questioning what life would be like if humankind performed tasks and attained goals by other means."[47]

Critically engaging with technology and media in a manner that notices their presence and effects, as well as thinking about whether default acceptance of those is necessary, becomes part of a life lived out faithfully in the world. Faithful living involves thinking about optimistic, pessimistic, and ambiguous responses to technology and how one might respond appropriately and wisely to the environment we find ourselves in.

A Starting Point for a Theology of Technology in an Age of Digital Media

Each of the responses identified above recognizes that the technological environment is all-embracing. Whether it be the vast vistas of possibility envisioned by the optimists; the bleak, oppressive world of technological determinism posited by the pessimists; or the ambiguity of those wrestling with technology, all agree that technology cannot be removed from human existence. Technology and media have become ingrained in our environment.

Thinking about technology as our environment raises interesting possibilities. Taking the notion of technology in an ecological sense, Bonnie Nardi and Vicki O'Day understand technology as "information ecology." They define information ecology as "a system of people, practices, values, and technologies in a particular local environment. In information ecologies, the spotlight is not on technology, but on human activities that are served by technology."[48] With connections to both global and local perspectives on the environment, this view of technology pays closer attention to contexts that shape technology's form and impact. Paying attention to the local context, as well as the wider social, economic, and political contexts encompassing the local, allows for different levels of granularity in technological engagement that move beyond an overwhelming global view of technology.[49]

Rather than focusing on tools, practices, and practitioners within technological systems, Nardi and O'Day shift the focus to the relationships between entities within a technological system. Technology becomes more than just a single tool for an individual and is instead examined as a network of relationships that responds to local environmental changes. From a theological perspective, this approach to technology allows the values and practices embedded within these relationships, as well as their effects upon people and the world they exist in, to be engaged through contextual theology. This occurs when the experiences of the technological environment in the present are in constant, faithful dialogue with the experience and contexts of the past found in sources such as Scripture and tradition and mediated through the material reality of the everyday world.[50]

Viewing technology ecologically recognizes technology as a dynamic and evolving system comprising diverse and interconnected entities and relationships. Change in one aspect of the system propagates through the system, altering relationships through feedback loops and altering the nature of the system, possibly rendering it unviable. Here we might find some useful overlap with the perspective on new media developed by Lev Manovich, who sees media and technology as caught up in a networked environment that creates feedback loops, which then shape the way that technology is used and developed. It is this feedback loop that puts the "new" in new media.[51]

By adjusting the scale at which relationships between entities such as tools or techniques are viewed, it is possible to identify certain entities as members of several different ecologies that may themselves be part of a single, larger ecosystem. A simple example is the way a company might have different kinds of computer networks operating in different geographic locations. Each local network connects to form a single company-wide computer network, which in turn is then connected to other organizations to form a yet larger network. The users, devices, software, and configurations of these networks are in a constant state of activity and change at these various levels. Moreover, this dynamic view of media and technology alerts us to the fact that technology and its components evolve over time. A technology may be ephemeral, existing in a particular time and place, or it may continue over time, as in the case of the book, being constantly refined or redefined. Likewise, new tools and methods arise to complement or replace existing ones, while people within the ecosystem adapt, or fail to adapt, to the new environment.[52]

Nardi and O'Day argue that focusing on technology as ecology brings urgency to our reflections, because it uses the language of environmental concern and awareness. Issues that deal with people, relationships, social justice, sustainability, and wise use of technology come to the fore, both in local and global contexts. This, in turn, provides a helpful avenue for connection with theological themes, recognizing that amid the network of relationships between tools, techniques, nature, and people, one might also find God and God's concerns. Furthermore, an ecological view of technology may provide novel ways of connecting theological concepts described using pastoral and agrarian metaphors with contemporary technological issues. As such, a definition of technology as a system of God, people, practices, values, and technological artifacts in a particular local environment serves as a useful starting place for theological engagement.

This chapter has highlighted some of the negotiation that has taken place around technology and media in the history of Christianity and that continues today. The Christian church has been both shaped by technology—for example, through its relationship with the Bible as a technological artifact—and has shaped the wider society with respect to technology and values surrounding it. In the process theologians have noted the emergence of three common reactions to technology and media reflecting optimistic, pessimistic, and ambiguous responses. For some, technology is tied to a God-given opportunity to make the world a better place, both materially and spiritually. For others, it represents something that has the capacity to dehumanize and break down authentic relationships between people and with the world. Finally, many individuals respond with considered ambiguity, in which the intentions and consequences of technology and media form an ever-shifting evaluation of their worth and effects.

Throughout this chapter we see a common theme developing, one that says that wisdom is needed to engage with and live within the technology and media that have become our environment. In future chapters we will address how we might approach the quest for that wisdom, what faithful and life-giving technology might look like, and how that technology can interact with our theologies of creation and humanity, with Christology, and with our hope for the future.

new media theory 101

Understanding New Media and the Network Society

Now that we have explored key perspectives and responses highlighted within theological inquiries of technology, we turn to the field of media studies. This chapter offers a crash course in new media theory to help readers understand the revolutionary components of digital media technologies and the values that they promote. To explain the "new" in new media, we will begin by outlining the difference between "old," traditional mass media and a new generation of digital, computer-network technologies. The chapter also discusses the rhetoric and innovations surrounding transitions from Web 1.0 to Web 3.0. This will enable us to more fully understand not just the unique features of new media technologies but also the key cultural traits these technologies promote and the social practices they facilitate. This will lead to a discussion about the image of the network and how its use in relation to network technologies and the network society reveals a new cultural lens. Thus, we will not only highlight certain technological innovations and characteristics but also show how these technologies create a set of expectations about how the digital world does and should function, opening up key ethical issues and concerns that these innovations raise for people of faith.

What Is New Media?

"New media" is a term used to describe a whole range of digital technologies and forms of media, including computers, the internet, cell phones and smartphones, social networking software, and digital recording devices. The notion of new media surfaced in the late 1990s as a way to describe what was seen as a new generation of digital and computer-based technologies (e.g., laptops and MP3 players) with unique attributes and to differentiate these from older, analog forms of mass media, especially electronic media such as television and radio. Analog media content is assembled, stored, and sent along a continuous transmission of information, such as a single track of music relayed as sound waves through a needle moving along the grooves of a record. In new media, data are stored in a digital binary code that must be translated by a computer. An MP3 music track stores sounds in a form that is read and encoded by a digital device that translates numbers into sounds.

The integration of computer technologies with mass media has forever changed the way we produce, consume, and interact with media. In many respects this transition, compared to other media transitions, has been rapid. Take, for example, Heidi's experience in the early 1990s. At that time she was pursuing a BA in communication, training to be a print and radio journalist. For the first three years of this training, she spent countless hours in the radio production lab recording stories and interviews on spools of magnetic tape set up on large reel-to-reel recording devices. Once a recording was made, she would carefully cue the tape to the interview snippet she wanted to include, and then use a razor blade to cut out sections of the recording and splice them together with special tape to create the final story. The process was time consuming and labor intensive and required attention to detail. If, by accident, a desired tape snippet fell to the floor or the tape was damaged, it could take hours to reassemble the story bit by bit.

When Heidi returned to college for her final year of courses, her professor announced on the first day of the advanced production course that the students' previous training was now obsolete. Students were shown a new computerized editing bay. Recordings were now captured by digital devices that replaced the complex hand-production process with a simple, more secure automated process. Sound recordings were now digitally encoded, saved, and stored on a computer. Razor blades and tape were replaced with mouse clicks as students cut-and-pasted to move sections of voice-overs on the screen. The professors led the students through a semester-long crash course on this new technology to get audio and video production skills up to the new industry standard. Digital production made the process quicker, more flexible, and much more forgiving; the ability to share content between projects added new possibilities to student radio and video projects. The digital aspect of new media had forever changed media production.

Although most technologies are now based on a computer infrastructure and digital media have become commonplace in our media landscape, the question is still often asked, "What is really 'new' about these newer forms of media?" Let us first consider the technically unique aspects of digital and computer-based technologies. Lev Manovich, in *The Language of New Media*, teases out what he considers to be the revolutionary character of new media technology, highlighting five technical characteristics that distinguish new media from older mass media technologies.[1] These characteristics include numerical representation, modularity, automation, variability, and transcoding.

Numerical Representation: Digitally Coded

First, new media are digitally coded. This means new media technologies are composed of numerical representations. In traditional mass media, like radio or television, media messages were composed of sound and light waves transmitted via antenna to devices that decoded these waves into music and pictures. In the digital age, sound and pictures are translated via computers into a binary code of 1s and 0s. Computers transfer and decode this digital data. Take, for example, the iPhone. When you take a picture with your iPhone, what you see on the screen is a discrete image. But the computer components of your smartphone read this image as a series of 1s and 0s that represent the codes for the different colors and shades that make up the picture on your screen. Because new media are based on numerical representation, they use a very different language than previous forms of media. DNA of new media is encoded to be read and interacted with via computer technology, giving it a unique framework for engagement and exchange.

Modularity: Digital Data as Building Block

Second, new media are modular. This means that the basic components of created new media content remain as discrete elements, so media content and information maintain separate identities. For example, in the era of analog music recordings, voices and instruments were recorded in such a way that the manipulation of these multiple tracks was more difficult and labor intensive. Now digital recording allows different voices and instruments to be recorded separately as distinct tracks or components that can be combined and mixed together through a digital editing bay into a single, seamless sound track. If you use a podcasting software program like Audacity or Camtasia, this becomes clear as background music, voices, or even images and video feeds are stored as separate tracks that can be added, cut, and manipulated separately before being saved together as a final sound/image track. Within new media, data can be stored together, yet each element retains its unique identity and can be manipulated separately. The result is that new media products are highly flexible and can easily be broken down into parts and recombined into new forms, leading to innovations in media composition such as mash-ups and remixes, discussed later in this chapter.

Automation: Programmable

Third, new media can be easily automated. This is because the digital encoding of new media offers a standard format or language for dealing with distinct forms of content (i.e., images, sound, and text). This standardization means that new media can be tagged and programmed so that files are automatically rendered in predetermined ways, allowing different forms of media to exist and interact similarly within a given media system. The ability to program how digital information is automatically rendered and saved removes part of the human element of control. For instance, instead of radio disc jockeys (DJs) carefully learning the music in their rotation and practicing how long they can or should talk over the introduction of a given song, such information is now provided automatically to the DJ and can even be controlled by voice-activation software. In this way the technology itself controls the DJ's voice-overs and dialogue on air. While new media offer new opportunities to preprogram features, such as how media are consumed and created, these opportunities are often computer dependent. This raises a range of issues about media authorship and authority, explored later in this chapter and the next.

Variability: Interactivity

Fourth, new media technologies are variable and easily changeable. This is because the standardization of media content through digital encoding translates previously diverse media languages (i.e., sound, image, and text) into a single numerical code. This numerical language system means new media content can be used for multiple media products and engaged in different ways simultaneously. Therefore, digital data becomes uniquely portable. New media images or texts can be easily copied, transferred to other devices, and used within different computerized interfaces simultaneously. Through digitization and modularity, new media contents become flexible, not locked into a single format or language as they were in previous mass-media forms. Digitized sound and images are both represented by numerical formulas on a computer, so any device with similar encoding capabilities can read and render this information appropriately. Instead of needing separate devices to decode music (an audio player), text (a screen), and photographic images (photo paper and chemicals), computer-readable content for different media forms can often be read on a single platform. Take again the variability of the iPhone, which decodes music via iTunes, captures pictures via a built-in digital camera, sends text messages, downloads websites, and handles phone calls. It is the flexibility of digital data that makes such transcoding possible.

Transcoding: A Multimedia Platform

Transcoding relates to the process of translating data and products into other or additional formats. Because they are based on 1s and 0s, new media are easily translated from one format to another. Take, for instance, a digital photograph. Once a digital image is captured, digital encoding allows it to be displayed in multiple forms simultaneously. Within moments of being downloaded, it can be posted on Facebook, become the new screensaver for your computer, be emailed to a friend who can print it, and even be uploaded to a website like Zazzle.com where you can produce a T-shirt with the picture on it. New media contents are not locked into one format or product; they can exist in a variety of forms or manipulations at the same time.

Although there is some overlap in these five characteristics of new media, we see through this overview that the current generation of computer-supported and coded technologies is much more flexible than previous media. Digital media can be stored, manipulated, and combined in ways not possible with previous audio or visual recordings. New media devices are much more robust and can deal with different forms of content simultaneously, rather than needing two content-specific devices to handle production and display separately. This move toward transcoding and modularity within the media device has important implications for future technologies, as seen in the rise and fall of the Flip Video camera, a simple digital high-definition recording device that came out in 2006 and was marketed by Pure Digital Technologies as a revolutionary handheld digital camcorder. The company was sold, and it was later shut down by its new owner, Cisco. One of the reasons given by Cisco was the rise of smartphones, which turned cell phones into multimedia devices, rendering Flip cameras obsolete because they duplicated recording features now standard on smartphones. The flexibility of new media both allows and pushes devices to be increasingly multipurpose.

Manovich sums up his discussion of the difference between old, analog media and new media with the following comparisons. In old or mass media, media space is considered static; television broadcasters or radio producers offer a set visual or oral story that the audience can either consume or ignore. In new media, media spaces are navigable. Digital content allows the audience to not only consume but also interact with different elements of the media in ways that can change perception of the message or even create a new version of that message.[2] These characteristics highlight the fact that new media are more dynamic, malleable, and programmable than the previous generation of analog media and are able to be personalized in ways that were not previously possible.

New media also encourage production processes that are highly interactive and audience generated. To describe this new phenomenon, some have used the term "prosumer," describing the idea of production by consumers. With the options for engagement made possible by the flexibility of digital media formats, audiences often become both the producers and the consumers of media content. The production potential within this generation of technologies also encourages distinctive patterns of user engagement. New media can be seen to foster a certain way of seeing reality and interacting with others. The flexibility of digital technologies offers potential for new collaborative engagement and creations. This allows new media to be both highly individualized, as content can be narrowcast to a defined set of users, and highly collaborative, encouraging the sharing of content and drawing from multiple sources simultaneously.

The Evolution of New Media in Web 1.0 to 3.0

Discussions of new media and digital technologies have become synonymous with the internet and the World Wide Web (WWW). The internet, the network of all connected networks, is an evolving set of technologies, which includes a variety of platforms and services, from email to websites to social media and virtual-world environments. The WWW, or "web," is the primary interface that people use to interact and connect with platforms and services offered by the internet. The web is a system of interlinked hypertext services allowing users to access webpages of text, image, and multimedia content. In the last decade, there has been much discussion about Web 2.0, highlighting unique social technologies and services that have made the internet even more accessible and driven by user-generated content. In the last few years, talk has emerged around Web 3.0, spotlighting a new generation of services and platforms further transforming the web landscape. These categories have become ways to describe the evolution of the internet and new media technologies and highlight the changing nature of user engagement through the network over the past two decades. Here we briefly discuss the move from Web 1.0 to 2.0 to 3.0 in order to contextualize how development of web technology has changed people's experience with and expectation of the internet.

Web 1.0

Web 1.0 is used to describe the earliest version of the internet as it was found in the beginning of the mid-1990s, when the internet first became accessible to a larger public audience. At this time the internet was equated with the WWW and webpages, and email was the most popular network activity. The internet opened up new opportunities for information gathering and making content available to a larger audience. However, creating a website still required certain levels of expertise and knowledge of computer languages such as HTML. This meant that most users were relegated to reading and searching for online content, and the creative production was in the hands of web professionals or webmasters with special training and skills. So, although the web was more interactive than previous forms of media and provided new opportunities for engagement, it was still in some respects a broadcast medium produced from the top down. One of the key innovations of the Web 1.0 era was the birth of portals and search engines, such as AskJeeves and Yahoo, which attempted to help users locate information online and find websites and people with shared interests. The Web 1.0 era saw the rise of information experts and curators, people who were skilled in helping users search or who could create resources to help users manage and collate the growing data put online. Web 1.0 dealt with information online in terms of its access and ability to allow personal engagement. Yet content was still only produced by a relatively select few, creating a new class of media professionals such as the webmaster, whose programming skills imparted control over the online environment.

Web 2.0

In the early 2000s, the term Web 2.0 arose as a way to describe a new range of services and possibilities online. Web 2.0 was used to highlight the rise of platforms that allowed internet users opportunities to more easily interact, collaborate, and create web content. For instance, blogging platforms such as LiveJournal.com and later Blogger.com enabled people to easily design and set up their own weblog within minutes, without needing to know HTML, and to program it with the desired functionality, such as archiving and enabling people to comment on posts. By the mid-2000s, we had seen the rise of wikis, podcasting, and video-sharing sites like YouTube that further allowed users to easily upload text, audio, and video content. The rise of social media platforms such as Facebook and Twitter not only facilitated the creation and sharing of user-generated content but also encouraged online conversation and social interaction on a new widespread scale.

While the web has always been an interactive medium, the Web 2.0 era moved the internet away from being dominated by the web professional and toward the prosumer. The web shifted from being a top-down enterprise to being a bottom-up endeavor that encouraged sharing content and conversation. For example, the YouTube platform not only allows users to publish videos but also creates communities of conversation through comments and frequent response videos to popular clips. The dynamic nature and flexibility of hundreds of new computer applications, such as Google, freely available online heightened the accessibility, reach, and usability of the internet. This era of social media gave rise to new web features—such as new forms of classification through searchable tags—that impacted the perception and presentation of online content. Such features increased the ability for critique and interaction through forum comments and reputation and aggregation services, creating new ways to evaluate and rank information.

Web 2.0 added a new level of interactivity to the internet, which some have argued has had a democratizing effect. The widening diffusion of the internet throughout the world, combined with the spread of participation platforms that lower the technical barriers to online engagement, means that Web 2.0 media technologies give voices to otherwise marginalized groups of people, such as young people and members of minority cultural and linguistic groups.[3]

Web 3.0

In the last few years the term Web 3.0 has arisen to highlight yet more changes currently occurring in the internet landscape. Although this categorization is still new and what it actually means is contested, a number of innovations and developments are often associated with discussions of Web 3.0.

One is the rise of cloud computing, which involves large groups of remote servers networked to allow centralized data storage so that users can store their data in a location where it can be accessed by multiple devices. Examples of this are file-sharing services such as GoogleDocs or Dropbox. Such file-hosting services allow users to store their files on their server networks rather than their own computer hard drives and then synchronize these files through client software so that users can access them in multiple locations. Because it is not tied to a single device, cloud computing offers users more freedom in how and where they access their data. This complements trends in mobile internet usage, as individuals increasingly access the internet where they are and when they want, rather than being tied to a specific device or space for access. Cloud computing signals a move in how data is stored and accessed by users, yet it raises questions about data ownership and privacy as users give up some control over their data to the owners of the remote server.

Also associated with Web 3.0 is the Semantic Web. This collaborative movement promotes the standardization of common data formats, computer languages, and the categorization of semantic content on websites. The internet, as the network of all connected networks, encompasses a variety of platforms and services with unique languages and ways of interacting. The aim of the Semantic Web is to create a common framework for how data is shared and reused across applications and groups, so that information can be interpreted by machines in a consistent manner. An example is creating consistencies in languages of search engines so that when you type in a word such as *foot*, the search engine knows whether you are looking for a part of the body or a distance of measurement based on other linguistic associations. Although the Semantic Web is still not fully realized, it marks a push toward addressing the current communication gap between human web users and computerized applications to create simpler and more consistent user interfaces and web experiences.

Another marker of Web 3.0 is the rise of the smart devices and mobile revolution, which highlights the increasing importance of mobile internet services and network capabilities no longer tied to a single device but embedded in multiple devices we carry with us. The smartphone exemplifies this trend. Internet users increasingly look for convergent digital devices, often portable and handheld, that combine multiple technologies and services and that can be used wherever and whenever they desire.

Also associated with Web 3.0, and pointing to what some are calling the coming markers of Web 4.0, are augmented reality (AR) technologies. AR links computer-generated sensory input, such as GPS data or infographics, to real-world environments, so that one's visual reality becomes augmented with additional digital information. This is illustrated by the development and testing of Google Glass, an image-recognition application device launched in spring 2012 that turned an Android operating system into an interactive optical recognition system. Through an optical head-mounted display designed like a pair of eyeglasses and using ubiquitous computer technology, an individual can take pictures of a physical environment and link those images to Google's online database. For example, if you take a picture of a building using Google Glass, the device will tell you what businesses are housed there, their opening hours, and other customer information. The Google Glass Project did not have the wide take-up initially hoped for, but this AR experiment points to the move toward making the internet a multisensory technology experience. Such enhancements and advancements raise interesting questions about how this and coming generations of internet technology will shape our perceptions of reality.

Overall, Web 3.0 represents the shift from a terrestrial to a mobile internet. With the proliferation of smartphones, people carry the internet with them, further widening the pervasiveness of the internet and its integration into daily tasks and routines. This trend is illustrated in an image circulated online comparing the 2005 crowd at Pope Benedict's papal enthronement straining to see the service from afar to the 2013 crowd alight with smartphones and tablets, attempting to document the event. New media are pervasive and part of our everyday routines. These new technologies promise greater levels of personalization, not just of the information accessed, but also of the experience afforded to users as they engage with a more standardized, dynamic, and convergent internet environment.

Understanding New Media Culture

The evolution of the internet and the attributes of new media discussed above not only point to the distinctive ways this generation of technologies are created and engaged; they also highlight underlying values that new media culture seems to promote. One of the highly praised values of new media, digital culture is interactivity. New media technologies offer interactive environments, allowing users to engage and create content and media products in faster and easier ways than previously possible. Such environments encourage new forms of media circulation and sociability as people share their creations (blog posts, Instagram images, etc.) online. Interactivity as a value is often framed as a space of potential freedom and creativity, especially for its users. The loosening of boundaries between creator and consumer through the rise of the prosumer creates a unique media landscape promoting a distinctive outlook. Manovich describes this in terms of "the ontology of the computer," meaning that the way computers function and encourage interaction can be seen to promote a certain value system.[4] This ontology encourages certain forms of social interactions.

One of the cultural beliefs promoted by new media culture, Manovich argues, is "meta-realism," a distinctive overarching view of reality that gives technology users similar standing and power as media authors or creators.[5] The flexibility of new media production means that users not only consume but also have power to deconstruct, control, and re-present the reality they are presented with in a given media product. Take, for instance, the rise of memes online.

The term "meme" was coined by Richard Dawkins to describe how ideas get passed virally and evolve within a culture, similar to how a virus mutates as it is passed from host to host. Memes are ideas that spread from person to person in a given culture and carry with them culturally meaningful ideas, symbols, or practices.

Internet memes are often based on a popular image or saying that is applied to a new context and shared online. This is seen in the popularity of LOLCats.com memes, where internet users incorporate playful images of cats with humorous sayings (such as the famous "I Can Has Cheezburger?" meme originally posted in 2007) that are then spoofed by other users. Because digital images found online can easily be copied, personalized, or incorporated into new messages, creating new versions of a popular meme is quick and easy. Meme generators such as QuickMeme.com or MemeGenerator.net give anyone with access to the internet the ability to combine a digital photo with a popular saying to create their own pun and post it online. Take, for instance, the multiple versions of the original red WWII poster with a crown and the slogan "Keep Calm and Carry On," initially created by the British government to encourage its citizens during war time. The Keep Calm meme has been co-opted by many people to create playful exhortations circulated online, from "Keep Calm and Dance On" to popular culture references such as the Star Wars–inspired "Keep Calm and Use the Force" to religious slogans like "Keep Calm and Follow Jesus." Internet memes show that the original creator of a message often has little control of the image and meaning once it is placed online. Internet memes are both communal, in that they involve sharing and evoke public discussion, and individual, being created and used in personal ways to communicate humor or make an identity statement.

Users of digital media can engage, manipulate, and bring their own interpretation to the reality they are presented with online. This is in contrast to the modernist, old-style realism of traditional mass media in which users could simply accept or reject the story or interpretation they were presented with in a media product. New media promote the assumption that the reality we perceive through an image, story, or sound track is flexible and not set. Prosumers are taught not to take what they are given at face value but rather to investigate, experiment with, and even change reality in light of their preferences. This shift advocates a very different system of authority for the new media audiences, one that empowers them to challenge the traditional media hierarchies and interpretations that come from established authorities. The media creator's power to have the final say on what a text or image means or represents potentially no longer exists. This move toward a flexible view of reality within new media culture also highlights a shift from set, prescribed narratives to stories and meanings that are, at their heart, interactive. This is a similar turn seen in other fields like literary theory where authorial intent is no longer seen as a given for interpreting meaning. Thus, some claim that new media teach us that nothing is ever final or complete and that there is always room for improvement.

Manovich argues that the character of new media presents us with a unique worldview. Old media were based on a linear view of the world in which technology was dependent upon a fixed, sequential logic determined by the media creators and bound by the system of production of a given medium. The audience could bring their own reading to a given film, television show, photograph, or book, but the media object itself was static. New media, however, are based on the logic of the database; one has access not only to reports rendered by the database but also the content that composes it. Now media content can be played with and reassembled to create new versions of a product. Thus, new media "create a cause and effect trajectory out of which seemingly unordered items and events find order."[6] In a database, emphasis is placed on each individual unit and its combination, displaying the narrative construct. Also in a database, meaning emerges from the relational links and connections made by the individual user rather than through a set, linear reading of the data itself. This database logic promotes the preferences of the user, encouraging individualized play over traveling down a predetermined path. For example, users can utilize the same search engines to draw different results through a slight modification of words and new personalization features that draw on previous searches and associations made by the users.

While old media provide a "window on the world" or present a set view of reality, new media offer users a "control panel" of multiple possibilities, with the ability to refract reality and create new versions of the world. This shift leads to a culture where the individual is empowered to critically engage with the nature of his or her collective reality in an intentional process of creation. New media technologies can be seen to encourage a user-centered approach, privileging creators and interpreters over traditional systems of authority and accountability. This is not to say that new media are always a solitary activity, for new media's push toward a participatory culture indeed encourages collaboration and interaction. However, the power given to the individual in new media culture changes traditional power relations.

Lest we think new media culture is a free-for-all, where users have the ultimate power to create and interpret, it is important to recognize that limits are embedded within new media culture, creating a paradox between freedom and control. Manovich discusses some of these limitations in terms of the "myth of interactivity."[7] Interactivity is a quality innate to the functionality of computers;

users are required to interact with the technology in order to draw information from the system to the visible screen. The media consumption process has become highly interactive; we choose not just what but also how we will engage with a given image or text. As seen above, digitization and the database structure of new media mean that users are able to control the paths and ways they interact with digital media content through the real-time manipulation of information displayed on the screen.

Although this interactive potential is often presented as a space of ultimate freedom and user control, it is not a space of complete freedom. Manovich argues that in some respects interactivity is a myth; new media are still a programmed environment. Take, for instance, someone interacting with a digital text online. The user is able to choose the order in which she will engage with the webpages of text, as hyperlinks allow her to explore other extracts of content embedded in the initial text or other sources associated with it. However, the user's range of options to explore that text has been preprogrammed by the creator of the digital text; that is, options for engagement are multiple but not infinite. The digital encoding does allow users to co-opt information or resources from a given text into their own version or media product, but they will need access to a digital platform that can accept and display that content. A blog, for instance, may allow users to copy and paste portions of digital text into their own narratives, provide hyperlinks to the text's online location, and incorporate text images as a blog post illustration. However, the possibilities for incorporation and engagement are again limited by the options and constraints offered by the designers of blog platforms and the flexibility of the code allowing users to create new options or modify display options. So, while digital media offer a much more flexible and varied environment, what they offer is a controlled interactivity.

In summary, new media culture can be seen to promote a meta-realism in which the world is a flexible space where reality can be created or manipulated. It offers database logic, which gives preference to the interpretive process of the individual user or user community over preestablished narratives. New media culture empowers individuals to act outside the confines of former institutional boundaries and to experiment, create, and share ideas in innovative ways. Yet it is also a culture of "controlled freedom" with built-in or invisible limits to this communicative expression and engagement. Such limits are based on the decisions and skills of technological elite and key web portals or tools such as Google. Thus, new media culture becomes a double-edged sword; it is a place of both empowerment and control. It is a space for new social engagement and community building and one that can promote the individual above the group.

The Conditions of Life in Network Society

So far we have discussed the unique character of digital media, the media practices this generation of technology encourages, and the narratives of reality and values they can be seen to support. New media lend themselves to creative adoption and allow users to become collaborators in media creation. This flexibility changes the power relationship between producer and consumer; media products are no longer seen as final cuts, but one version among many possibilities (e.g., "your truth" or "my truth"). This also changes underlying assumptions about how meaning is constructed and who holds interpretative authority over messages.

We have also considered how the metaphor of the network has become an important conceptual tool that emphasizes a new view of society and social structures that are changeable, decentralized, and based on personal preferences. Our social networks in a network society become both highly interconnected and highly individualized. The image of the network, as a space that contains both promise and peril, carries this paradox with it. Technology offers us visions of hope and fear for the future.

The tensions and realities in digital media and culture have led to a number of social developments. The developments can be seen as conditions of network society, in which digital technologies and their supporting culture encourage media engagement and behaviors with ethical implications. These conditions also pose challenges for people of faith, pointing toward theological issues regarding the human relationship to technology. Several of these conditions are discussed here and will be picked up again in chapter 4, which explores issues raised by the theology of technology in more depth.

Remix Culture

Digitization allows media content to be easily downloaded and integrated into multiple media platforms. This encourages the mixing of images, text, and sound, which become flexible building blocks for new media creations. This process is often referred to as a remix or a mash-up. A remix is a reinterpretation or re-creation of a preexisting form of media; it retains the aura in the initial story, image, or recording but is combined with new components in a novel order so that it is, in essence, a new creation. A mash-up is an extension of remixing; it is the sampling of different kinds of media, which are uniquely combined into a single format to make a new media product.

The concept of mashing up and remixing media comes from the music scene, with roots in disco, hip-hop culture, and the work of the DJ. In this context, the DJ uses turntables, sound systems, songs, and sounds to create a seamless performance of music. For the DJ, "the true art lies in the 'mix'" and the ability to combine preexisting recordings into new musical experiences, either in the studio or at live events.[8] In the club, the DJ aims to create a vibe, an ambient experience, by using sound, light, and even screened images to transform the club into an experiential public space. Here individuals can move either alone or together in the rhythm of a carefully constructed media environment. In the studio, the DJ combines segments from previous recordings into a new combination to create a new song and new experiences of the music, called a remix.

Today remixes and mash-ups have become a core part of new media culture. Various online software allows the average user to cut and paste static or moving images, sound tracks, and text into his or her own mash-up videos or remixed images, which can then be put on display on websites like YouTube or published on a personal blog. New media technology provides professionals and amateur digital creatives with tools, enabling them to reassemble digital content into images and spaces that offer new interpretations and expressions of the original content and associated meanings.

This ability to break down a visual or audio text into individual elements and symbols and reassemble them into a new narrative empowers individual creativity. The remix culture encourages experimentation and reinterpretation, as any digital content offers a never-ending stream of possible presentations. Remix and mash-up involve a unique type of creativity involving the ability to reflect, select, and extend the original text. Expertise is based on the ability to manipulate and modify a previous medium. Authority is based on allegory, demonstrating an ability to reflect a preexisting text or image but adapting it into something distinct that tells a new story. There are limits to this creativity, however. Because popular video clips, images, and text may be constrained under digital copyright laws, some remixes may be illegal and removed from public sites such as YouTube or Pinterest when there is a violation.

New media culture is not always based on remix, yet the mixing and manipulation of information, facilitated through digital technologies, is a common part of new media landscapes. Remixes and mash-ups support Manovich's idea of a meta-reality that emphasizes production processes, multiple versions, and the recirculation of ideas over final products and meaning. Remix culture has potentially serious implications for how we understand the role of the individual, community, and authority in society. Remix culture provides new possibilities for multiauthored collaboration and alternative voices, empowering some, yet simultaneously undermining traditional interpretative patterns and authorities. These issues are further explored in chapter 6.

Constant Contact

Research has shown that our ability to be in immediate contact with our chosen social network is ushering in broad social changes. The rise of mobile and smart media has seemingly led to a culture of constant contact. The instantaneous nature of email communication quickly taught us that the internet allows us to easily transcend time-space boundaries and connect with people anytime and anywhere there is a network connection. The web and search engines taught us that facts and data are available to us with a few keystrokes. We no longer have to go to a physical location, like a library or even a book, to look for specific information; it comes directly to us through the internet. The rise of chat software such as Skype has further taught us that instantaneous, synchronous, and in many cases free communication with others is available to us at our convenience. The proliferation of smartphones means we now have access to our social networks and data tools wherever we are. These innovations provide us with both a growing expectation of connecting with—and the ability to connect with—people and information whenever we want and on our own terms.

This connectivity has led to two important trends. The first is an "always on" response toward technology. With easy and cheap access to network technologies, at least in urban Western society, people have grown accustomed to the ability to be in contact with whom and what they want, whenever they want. This ability is heightened by the prevalence of smartphones and a mobile internet. Our handsets have become multimedia devices through which we can continuously interact with work, entertainment, and information anywhere we can find a signal. This has created expectations that people should be instantly accessible and that we should immediately be able to gain access or respond to the content or people. Public spaces often host seemingly private conversations. Traditionally noncommunicative spaces, from cars to church services, are often interrupted and have been transformed into social arenas. It is now users' preference and not traditional sociocultural boundaries that sets communicative expectations. Some people now sleep with their cell phones under their pillows, keeping a line open to loved ones. Some teens set up live webcams so they can "sleep" with their girlfriends or boyfriends and stay connected through the night. Personal desires to stay connected to and through technology are causing shifts in previously established boundaries for public-private interactions. The only limits to the desire to be always on often seem to be the technological limits of our devices and the need to access power sources at regular intervals to recharge the batteries of our always-on devices.

Second, the expectation of being always on has encouraged a distinctive attitude toward communication connectivity. For many, the ability to be connected to the internet and mobile networks is not seen as a simple benefit of life in our wired world; rather, it is seen as a right. Our relationship to information has changed, as we are often not expected to have to possess or know certain forms of information ahead of time, as was previously expected. For instance, instead of getting a map to find a place, we expect to be able to check our location via a mobile maps app, and instead of setting a time to meet a friend, we expect to be able to text them and make such arrangements when needed. When information is expected to be available on our own timetables and at our convenience, it eliminates the need for preparatory learning or knowledge acquisition.

Connectivity is seen no longer as an act but as a value, something of intrinsic worth. We expect to be able to connect on our own terms, in light of personal needs and desires. Many of our daily routines and work tasks and patterns are based on the assumption of connectivity. When we are unable to connect to the network, when our internet connection or cell phone reception fails, we often become cross or temporarily paralyzed. When information or access is unavailable, the result is often confusion and disorientation—for example, the feeling of loss when one's computer breaks down or internet access goes out in the workplace. Such reactions are due not only to the inconvenience but also to a breakdown in our social structures, cultural expectations, and patterns of being. In my (Heidi's) classes, I require students to shut off or at least silence and stow away their phones so they are not visible. For many students, my asking this is like asking them not to breathe for an hour. "But what if someone needs to get ahold of me?" they often ask. I remind them that not too many years ago, one would have to search out a landline or pay telephone to make a call.

As we have seen, the expectation of constant contact has changed people's perspective toward communication, with more and more people viewing access to digital media as a right. This rights language is especially evident in recent debates over net neutrality as the US government and telecoms have proposed a tiered internet service of a fast and slow lane for data exchange, so that consumers might have to pay more for steady and reliable bandwidth. While many view cheap and constant internet access as a communication right, it is important to recognize that the infrastructure of networks is owned by corporations who hold control and influence over users. In addition to being perceived as a human right, connectivity can be seen as a commodity, pointing toward assumptions underlying new media cultural values; this topic will be discussed further in following chapters.

Individualized Control

Another condition emerging from the network society is a shift in our understanding of how relationships are constituted. Network society is based on a social-technical infrastructure, which means that relationships are most often mediated through various technologies and social infrastructures. This mediation introduces new expectations of social separation between people, because communication frequently occurs through technological outlets that favor the individual communicative preference over the shared communication space of face-to-face dialogue.

The approach to community based on social network analysis argues that the individual rather than institutions is now the central node or media hub within networked communication. For example, in *The Internet in Everyday Life*, Wellman and Haythornthwaite affirm that the "personalization" and "portability" of online communication promotes a networked individualism, meaning that the basis for community and connectivity is individuals and not households or groups.[9] This move creates an expectation of personally oriented communities and ego-centered networks, which may seem to run counter to perceived traditional communal virtues of accountability and privileging communal needs over those of the individual. In *Smart Mobs*, which maps new forms of gathering in digital culture and the move toward crowdsourcing, Rheingold asserts that individuals connect with "multiple social milieus with limited involvement in each one," which "diminishes the control each milieu exercises over the individuals and decreases its commitment to the individual's welfare."[10] This suggests that people's motivations for using a technological network as a social network might be primarily for their personal benefit.

Van Djik similarly observes that online communities are focused on special interests, drawing together people who possess a shared point of interest and leading to an easily generalized identity.[11] Although the people represent heterogeneous groupings apart from their shared interests, these interests create more homogeneous groupings and a greater opportunity for members to build a shared identity and culture. It can be argued that by encouraging specialized and selective relationships, creators of online technology can manipulate and control various social settings. Although this does not mean that all online communication and networks are strictly inward-looking or self-motivated, it suggests that it is crucial to reflect on how online and mobile technologies shape our understanding of relationships. We suggest that the extent to which network technologies promote and encourage individualized forms of control has potential implications for the moral discourse and practices promoted within network culture.

Publicized Privacy

Finally, an important by-product of constant contact and highly individualized engagement online is the blurring of public and private boundaries. Increasing amounts of our personal information are shared, intentionally and unintentionally, and accessible online. This is partially due to the fact that public records and factual data, once available only through governmental offices and written requests, are now stored and readily searchable in various online repositories. This has led to the emergence of a crop of personal data websites, such as Zabasearch.com, 123people.com or Spokeo.com, where for free or a small price one can easily access aggregated personal details (e.g., current address, work history, even social security number) on almost any individual.

Social network sites such as Twitter, Facebook, and Pinterest have become places that encourage people to share personal preferences, updates, and beliefs with a network of personal contacts or those with similar interests. Though such spaces may appear to be private, where information is shared among friends, because of the tenuous nature of privacy settings and the fact that data such as tweets are publicly archived, what is perceived as private is often a publicly accessible data trail of individual preferences and patterns of behavior. Thus, new media culture has led to changing, even disappearing, boundaries between private and public life. Some argue that a lack of privacy should always be assumed when one chooses to live any part of one's life online, and that all life is public in a network society. However, this reconfiguring of traditional public-private boundaries has broad cultural and social implications, especially for issues that were once considered private matters, such as political and religious affiliations. Digital culture easily reveals that which we wish to keep personal and private, which can have both positive outcomes, such as revealing deception, as well as problematic ones.

This trend has been described as "publicized privacy," as online contexts erode the physical markers of private space. For instance, in mobile and cell phone culture, once private conversation often takes place in very public spaces (buses, coffee shops, on the street), turning personal phone exchanges into public spectacles. This means that much of what was once private communication becomes a public performance. John Sloop and Joshua Gunn define publicized privacy as the conditions created when new communication technologies "create an ideology and sensation of freedom that ironically leads to heightened states of surveillance and discipline."[12]

The paradox of publicized privacy is that, on the one hand, new media culture offers unique opportunities to voice one's opinion or personally respond to topics one is passionate about. In the case of religion, new media can be easily leveraged to articulate one's faith and convictions to a global audience. Sites like YouTube provide a public platform for apologetics, evangelism, and spiritual storytelling; and the digital archiving and sharing of such media means that the influence and reach of a video clip can extend far beyond the social reach and personal network of any one person. Yet because life online is in many respects always a public performance not completely under one's control, one's digital storytelling and sharing can easily be monitored, manipulated, or co-opted into other unauthorized versions. Once it is placed online, one's text, photo, or story is no longer a personal but a public and malleable artifact. This means individuals must always be aware and engage in the interpretation and oversight of the personal presentations online, encouraging an "always on" behavior.

So the fantasy of freedom is replaced by the threat of exposure or manipulation, as new media encourage compulsive sharing of personal experience, status, and location. This requires people to develop skills in managing their mediated, very public personal expression, even when it is perceived to be private. Publicized privacy raises many questions about what religious content should or should not be shared online and how one should live out personal spirituality in such an environment. Together, the conditions of network society pose a range of challenges and opportunities for people of faith, which will be explored further in chapter 4.

Summarizing the Nature of New Media

The unique features of new media offer users a more dynamic, varied, and self-regulated form of engagement than the previous generation of analog media. Both the technical features and social patterns they encourage are having a significant impact on society. We have noted the rise of a network society, where community and relationships are seen as fluid and changing, dependent on the needs of the individual. Geography becomes irrelevant as time-space barriers dissolve between people and information. A new social structure emerges where the networked individual becomes the center point of the social system, which endows people with new freedom to create their own need- and preference-based networks, while challenging traditional family and institutional relationships. In this new reality offered by digital technologies and the society entwined in them, conventional understandings of hierarchy, identity, and community are being reconfigured, raising many social, cultural, and spiritual questions.

This chapter argues that understanding new media helps us understand the roots of a set of cultural beliefs that these technologies seem to promote. Although we argue that new media like computers and other digital media are not neutral, carrying with them certain preferences and encouraging certain patterns, we see the values and pathways they promote as a given. Our analysis of digital technology and culture is presented here to reveal some of the hidden assumptions and priorities in the new media landscape.

While new media are having a significant influence on creative and social structures, we do not want to suggest that these technologies are overpowering. We do not assume that new media represent an all-powerful force, implanting their values on everything they touch. As will be shown in the following chapter, the flexibility of new media means users have the ability to influence the shape, impact, and outcomes of digital technologies in a variety of social spaces. Digital users adopt the technology for their own purposes, and these intentions can alter the nature of the technology, leading to new values and outcomes. Because digital technologies empower people to manipulate structures and meanings, they can also be cultured in light of religious belief and intentions. Therefore, we must understand the structure of different media platforms, the intent of the designers, and the user community surrounding these technologies.[13]

networked religion

Considering How Faith Is Lived in a Network Society

Over the past few decades there has been much speculation about the transformative nature of the internet, with many predictions about how it would transform all areas of life, including the ways we practice religion. Indeed, the internet has provided many new opportunities for people to connect inside and outside the church, do ministry, evangelize, and even structure worship. Examples of online worship services, sermons via Twitter, and mission mobilization through Facebook abound. However, while digital media offer unique ways of doing church, integrating digital media into a worship service or religious education does not necessarily mean that Christian practice is completely transformed. As the internet has been integrated more and more into our daily and spiritual routines, there is a growing awareness that new media practices are becoming embedded in the everyday. This means online and offline religious practices are often intimately connected, as prayers sent via email or posted on Facebook are seen as part of one's overall prayer life rather than as a separate act or context.

In fact, many people who study religious practice online, a field that has become known as Digital Religion studies,[1] have found that close observation of the way people use the internet for religious purposes may reveal wider trends in how religious practice is seen and manifested in broader offline contexts.

This chapter explores how people use the internet for religious purposes in order to show how these trends mirror larger shifts in contemporary religious practice offline. While the research presented here speaks more broadly about the myriad ways religion is manifest online, we will show how these trends have direct implications for Christianity and Christian communities. We argue that careful attention to how religion is seen online can teach us about how people's faith is manifested and informed by the structures and culture of network society in general. It also reveals the specific ways new media technologies may shape the practices of people of faith and reflect changing assumptions about the nature of our spiritual lives.

We begin by considering the rise of religious practice online, providing an overview of Christian use of the internet over the past three decades. This leads us to identifying key characteristics of how people practice religion online. Networked religion is introduced as a concept that highlights how religion has been informed by the nature of the network society and the social-technical structures that support it. The five key traits of networked religion are discussed in detail in order to consider what religious practices online teach us about the cultural values and spiritual trends in the new media landscape. These traits have important implications for the Christian community and faith.

The Rise of Religion Online

For over three decades the internet has been used for a variety of religious practices and activities. Beginning in the early 1980s, religious computer enthusiasts brought their faith online in newsgroups and formed online communities, such as the net.religion group formed circa 1984, via email and Usenet. Early religious internet users also experimented with new forms of religious communication and connection, such as the first recorded Christian email newsletter, "United Methodist Information," launched in the late 1980s. In the 1990s, increasing numbers of religious groups and mailing lists began to emerge online, such as Ecunet (www.ecunet.org), an ecumenical Christian email listserv. Early in this decade, the first Christian online congregation, The First Church of Cyberspace, was established by American Presbyterians. For over a decade they held a weekly service via IRC chat and offered web interaction for participants (www.godweb.org). In 1996 *Time* magazine published a special issue on religion online, highlighting the dozens of religious websites and online resources, from the first monastic website, Monastery of Christ in the Desert (www.christdesert.org), which gave monks in remote places access to an international audience for ministry, to the Virtual Memorial Garden (catless.ncl.ac.uk/vmg/), where people created digital tributes to people and pets that had passed away.

Throughout the 1990s, people from traditional and nontraditional religions experimented with creating new religious resources online. For example, Gospelcom (www.gospelcom.net) provided Christians with access to online Bible-study tools and various interactive devotional and fellowship groups. In the late 1990s, interreligious information hubs such as Beliefnet (www.beliefnet.org) emerged online, offering everything from thoughts for the day from the pope to inspirational screensavers and access to sacred texts. By the 2000s religion online had become commonplace on the internet's landscape. Blogging platforms such as LiveJournal and Blogger.com allowed religious blogs and blog hubs to emerge, such as Christian Bloggy Moms (www.bloggymoms.com) hosting Christian mommy blogger pages and The Gospel Coalition (http://thegospelcoalition.org/blogs) offering Christians a common space to blog about their faith. The rise of podcasting led to a revolution in "godcasting," or audio and visual broadcasting of religious talk shows from televangelists to homeschool moms (e.g., The GodCast Network [www.godcast.org] and GODcasting.tv [www.godcasting.tv]).

The rise of virtual world environments in the mid-2000s similarly birthed experiments in religious worship, for example, the Church of Fools (www.churchoffools.com), a short-lived online (3-D) church experiment sponsored by the Methodist Church of Britain, and the satirical website Ship of Fools and its offshoot St Pixels: Church of the Internet (www.stpixels.com), offering chat rooms and a "real-time" online worship forum to its members. Both examples challenged the notion of what it means to be a church in a digital age. The emergence of Second Life (http://secondlife.com), a 3-D virtual world allowing residents to interact via a motional avatar to socialize, play, create, and do business with other virtual residents, created room for people to reimagine religious locations in digital spaces. Online people soon began to experiment with translating and importing their religious practice into the digital space, including creating prayer and church services at one of numerous Second Life worship spaces such as the ALM Cyberchurch, the Anglican Cathedral in Second Life, or Life Church's Second Life campus.

By the late 2000s, social media had replaced email as the number one activity online. Christian users began to populate spaces such as MySpace, Facebook, and later Twitter, using these new forms of social interaction as opportunities to publicize their faith or create novel forms of religious engagement. One can now find multiple Facebook accounts and even tweets for Jesus. Some religious groups have become concerned about the negative side of social networking exposing their members to secular values or problematic sexual content. This concern has led to the creation of religious versions of popular social networking sites such as MyChurch.org and Xiaz.com. Religious versions of the video sharing website YouTube.com have also been launched (e.g., GodTube .com), offering alternative venues for religious believers to participate in the same activities offered by popular sites but in the context of a community of like-minded believers. More recently, platforms such as Instagram and Pinterest have become spaces to share devotional images and Scripture in ways that are easily spreadable through social media and to seek to inspire Christians in their faith and core beliefs.

The internet has also afforded creative opportunities to incorporate the internet in Christian mission. Groups such as the Global Christian Internet Alliance and Internet Evangelism Coalition formed to share resources and strategies about online ministry, and now groups such as the Mobile Ministry Forum bring together Christian ministries and developers to discuss how smart and mobile technologies can be used for Christian evangelism and education. As we have seen, Christians have adopted the internet for a variety of purposes and religious ends, and creating a presence online has become a vital way to connect spiritual seekers in digital culture.

Defining Networked Religion

As we have already discussed, the image of the network points to a number of assumptions about the nature of the network society and culture. Network society is based on social relationships that are flexible rather than fixed. These relationships are loosely connected by needs and preference rather than tightly connected by tradition and institutions. The internet as a network empowers individuals and encourages new forms of interaction like crowdsourced problem solving and global resource sharing. It also presents digital technologies as dichotomous, meaning that they present opportunities and challenges for how we relate to others. The image of the network further emphasizes that societal structures, and even our social relationships, are increasingly decentralized yet interconnected and supported by a social-technical infrastructure. The network-based society is seen to shape all areas of society, from the political and economic worlds to the religious world. We argue that, in light of this, it is important to consider what kind of religious culture and landscape is being facilitated by network society.

Here we explore a conception of religion informed by the technological structures and characteristics of the internet such as flattening of traditional hierarchies (encouraging instantaneous communication and response) and widening access to sacred or once private information. It is clear that the forms of religious practice emerging online have been marked by these characteristics of our computer-based network society. As we will discuss, not only individuals but also religious institutions are being forced to adapt and alter their traditional forms of connection, hierarchy, and religious-identity presentation as these practices are transported online.

We introduce the concept of networked religion not only to highlight the ways people practice religion online but also to show how trends within religion reveal cultural changes in popular understandings of religion in broader society.[2] The idea of networked religion suggests that religion, which is found online and offline, is informed by the structures, practices, and character of network society. Networked religion is defined by five key traits: networked community, storied identities, convergent practices, shifting authority, and a multisite reality. These traits highlight common attributes of what scholars have learned about how religion is practiced online. These attributes are explored in detail in this chapter—illustrating important trends in a network society with regard to the practice of religion, especially Christianity, that are important for us to consider in order to understand the influence of new media culture on religious beliefs and behaviors.

Networked Community

We begin our exploration of religion looking at the characteristics of networked community. Online communities exist as loose social networks where members have varying levels of affiliation and commitment. This is in contrast to traditional communities, which often exist as more tightly bounded social structures overseen by family and institutional ties. Online religious communities often function quite differently than conventional religious groups and institutions, where membership is established through a set of rituals such as confirmation, baptism, or an act of public confession. Online religious communities are often formed through people's commitment to a shared interest, and membership is based on active participation in group conversation and online activities rather than affiliation or membership rituals.

As seen above, since the late 1990s networked community has had many faces online, reflecting the diversity of platforms on which it has existed. Online communities typically share common traits, including exhibiting dynamic connections between members who share interests and creating a network of relations and commitments that change on the basis of the composition and commitment of the community at a given time. Take, for example, the Anglican Cathedral in Second Life, an online church community drawing some four hundred participants to its multiple weekly meetings. This group has sought to create a space where participants can build personal social connections with others online. The virtual cathedral has also built links to the larger Anglican community to help solidify the community ethos it seeks to cultivate.[3] Participants have praised this community for offering higher levels of control over the environment and the individual's extent of social engagement than afforded in offline churches.[4] Thus, the Anglican Cathedral in Second Life offers the potential of an individualized communal experience, which expresses traits of networked community as members' involvement and investment vary in their degree of depth and affiliation.

Much research has been conducted on people's motivation for joining and investing in online communities and how online participation might affect one's engagement in or perceptions of offline community. Early Digital Religion studies in the 1990s explored how people seek to create community in an unbounded space, raising questions regarding what was seen as the blurring of traditional social boundaries online in regard to community leadership, rule making, changes in behavioral expectation, and how these groups are described.[5] Researchers noted that online communities were often marked by shared characteristics or values that drew users to specific online groups.[6] Online communities are personalized social networks of shared interest, allowing individuals to choose the extent of their involvement and connect multiple social contexts simultaneously.

Studies of Christian community online have found that theological orientation or religious identity often draws members together. Researchers noted that new patterns of social sharing and interaction online may lead to shifts in expectations regarding the nature of community.[7] The ability to interact and exchange ideas with people from different parts of the world from a shared-faith perspective can transform members' expectations of how contemporary religious groups could or should function. These expectations create desires for online Christian community members to experiment with and even model in their offline churches new styles of small-group interaction, accountability networks, or forms of dialogue experienced online. Thus, rather than simply critique online community as problematic because it is new and different, researchers suggest it should be carefully studied to see what new definitions of church and hopes for religious culture may arise within the practices of online Christian communities.

While some Christians and church leaders have voiced concern that online community might encourage people to "plug in, log on, and drop out" of offline communities, current research does not support such fears. Studies have found that while online communities encourage new ways of gathering and new social behaviors, they generally serve as a supplement, not a substitute, for offline church involvement.[8] People may join an online community to meet specific relational or informational needs, such as in-depth Bible study or spiritual support, yet this involvement augments and is in addition to, rather than a replacement for, an embodied, offline worship experience. In some cases, new patterns of behavior learned or experienced online regarding prayer support and accountability may even become a template for how small groups function offline.

These findings reveal a close connection between online and offline community. For instance, studies of denominational websites and forms of online church are often closely connected to offline Christianity and the institutions they represent, even when traditional communal rituals and practices (e.g., prayer or Bible study) are modified online.[9] The network nature of community online allows members to bridge their online and offline spiritual activities to build a cohesive spiritual network of commitments and practices. The network, as previously noted, provides a metaphor to show how individuals and groups seek to describe and connect their spiritual lives in a much more global and fluid nature of contemporary social relations. Increasingly, religious communities online and offline mirror this trend toward loose social networks with varying levels of affiliation and commitment. Recent studies by the Pew Foundation have found that young people are increasingly resisting formal or traditional affiliations with churches and religious institutions but may still have personal desires for religious connection and involvement. Young people often have multiple involvements of varying depth in a variety of groups, allowing them to move between and explore different forms of religious experience without holding firm commitments to any one group or ideological orientation.[10]

The concept of networked community provides a valuable lens for describing the function of community both online and offline, especially within contemporary Western society. The study of online religious communities spotlights the fact that rather than living in a single static religious community, many people in contemporary society live in religious social networks that are emergent, varying in depth, fluid, and highly personalized.

Storied Identity

Closely tied to our understanding of religious community is our understanding of religious identity. Identity is a unique collection of characteristics by which something is identified or someone is known. Religious identity represents the core characteristics or values with which a religious group or individual identifies as a way to distinguish themselves from others.

Traditionally, studies of religion have been concerned with the integration, consolidation, and control of certain religious identities within specific groups and institutions. Yet the mediation of social relations online often bypasses traditional structures of identity formation, adding new complexities to such studies. It is clear from current research that religious identity is not simply absorbed through the internet, nor is it purely imported from the offline context. Identity online is highly malleable rather than fixed. Increasingly the internet is seen as one of a number of tools empowering individuals to act out their identities in unique ways in contemporary society. Identity online often becomes an act of conscious performance, in which individuals select, assemble, and present their senses of self through a variety of resources available to them. Internet users engage with blogs, webpages, and forums to seek out religious information and experiences and then use this to reflect on their responses. The information, images, and experiences they collect and engage with help individuals work out and express their religious selves online as they incorporate them into their online profiles and the spaces they participate in. Therefore, the internet provides the resources and space that help religious individuals explore and present the beliefs and values they identify with. In this way the internet becomes a tool to perform the religious persona they seek to portray to the online public.

This ability and freedom to create and present one's religious identity show that it is both constructed and performed online. The notion of storied identity highlights the fact that internet users often draw from multiple sources as they seek to create and present self-assembled spiritual identities online. These processes of construction and performance are central within online identity creation. The temporal nature of online spaces and information often leads people to seek out a storied identity in an attempt to create coherence amid the fluidity of the internet. Here the self may be assembled through a variety of resources, such as quoting commentary from one's favorite religious website, providing links to an inspirational godcast, and posting internet memes that express key convictions. When these are grouped together, say on one's social media account, they present a distinctive narrative about an individual's beliefs and what he or she stands for.

The creation of a storied identity online can be clearly seen in the practices of many religious bloggers. Blogging involves individuals who keep an online journal often focused on personal content or opinions and typically intended for a public audience. Blogs can cover a multitude of themes, from parental advice offered by "mommy bloggers" or citizen journalism bloggers offering news reporting and commentaries to "theoblogians" who blog on issues of faith and biblical interpretation. Research has found that bloggers frequently write about their faith practices by chronicling their spiritual journey, offering a prophetic voice in relation to a personally defined religious mission or using the forum for apologetics and occasionally for venting on religious debates.[11] In many respects, religious blogging becomes about constructing and performing a specific religious identity online in making public one's process of religious self-identification. This is done by framing blogging practice in religious terms, such as affiliating with religious blog networks or tagging the use of religious terminology, so that posts or blogger profiles are linked via searches to certain identity markers. A blogger's storied identity emerges through religious connections and choices made online, such as highlighting institutional and faith group affiliations in their postings or adding a links list to their blog. Religious bloggers may serve as armchair theologians or cultural critics as they selectively affirm their preferred religious authorities or texts and stress the ways these coalesce into or diverge from their personal beliefs. This shows that religious bloggers shape the blogosphere according to their personalized understandings of spirituality, so religious blogging is simultaneously both community oriented and individualized.

Early researchers of religion online became concerned about what function traditional religious structures could continue to play in this new process of identity construction in an increasingly globalized, network society. The internet has been praised by some because it offers unique opportunities that empower religious individuals. With easy online access to religious texts and a variety of interpretative tools, people no longer have to go through established religious teachers or structures for such information.[12] The internet provides new possibilities for building and presenting one's religious identity. This is especially true for people who lack such opportunities in their local offline context or belong to fringe groups that may face higher degrees of public scrutiny.[13] The internet also becomes a tool to present one's religious identity in ways that are less structured than avenues often offered by institutions. Online, one can bypass expected initiation or training rites to become an instant religious expert. One builds an online reputation through credibility gained by the number of "fans," "likes," or "retweets" collected.

Yet others have voiced concerns about anonymity and the transient nature of online interactions, which may bring unintended consequences. These include a potential identity fragmentation as people are encouraged to experiment rather than establish a fixed identity. This experimentation can lead to conflicts between the truth claims of online religious authorities and their offline counterparts. Some have suggested that such experiences can inhibit an individual's ability to develop a cohesive religious identity or restrict one's reaffirmation of accepted boundaries between traditional and personal religious identity. For example, sociologist of religion Mia Lövheim found that young Swedish

Christians seeking to present their personalized faith narratives online struggled with what they perceived as authentic religious identities, created through their online engagement, and those that traditional religious leaders might interpret as fake or unsanctioned.[14] This highlights a disconnect experienced by many between religious identity experiences in the everyday realities of networked life and the prescribed definitions and expectations long established by offline religious communities.

Despite this tension, it is important to note that those who study the social impact of the internet find that religious identity online is not separated from an individual's identity in life outside the internet.[15] People often work hard to create what is perceived as an authentic online presence that complements their offline persona or mirrors the image of themselves they seek to portray across media. The internet becomes a place for building one's religious self through experimentation with different ways of being and the adoption of traditional identity roles. Scholars have found that internet users tend to create online identities that closely resemble or are connected to traits found in their offline identities.[16] Internet users also evaluate others' identities online on the basis of, and ascribe them to, their offline beliefs and even common stereotypes such as gender or race.[17] Paying attention to the nature of online environments becomes important for understanding how identity performance in such spaces develops within an individual's everyday life and acts as a foundation for building offline relationships and attitudes.[18] Thus, identity online, both in religious and nonreligious contexts, creates new, dynamic opportunities for self-expression of belief and lifestyle, presenting identity as a process of performance.

Religious identity as a storied identity acknowledges that identity construction is a process lived out online and offline, created in an attempt to bring connection between different spheres of interaction and the Christian narrative of faith. It also suggests that spiritual identity formation is seen as a continuous process in which people strive for coherence and authenticity between their convictions and conduct.

Convergent Practice

One of the clearest markers of digital religion is the way people of faith transport and transform specific religious practices online. Religious rituals, such as prayer and religious study, are important distinguishing factors of religious identity. By whom, when, and how a given religious practice is to be performed is often carefully scripted and based on the theological interpretations and historical or cultural traditions of a given group. For instance, the act of Communion is a weekly ritual for some Christian groups and a quarterly practice for others because of specific traditions of interpretation of Christ's mandate to practice this holy meal when believers gather. However, online we see the reimaging of many traditional Christian rituals, such as worship in virtual-reality environments where one can light a digital candle as part of the practice. Early studies of religion online found that religious adopters of the internet readily defined it as a potential new sacred space to justify importing rituals online and creating new forms of religiosity in the space.[19] Since the mid-1990s, we have seen many creative expressions of traditional offline Christian practice move online, including the adaptation of prayer meetings in online environments,[20] the creation of cyber-altars or chapels,[21] and the performance of religious ceremonies and worship services.[22]

As individuals and groups create these new environments for religious devotion online, we see the mimicking and modification of many established practices. A common observation has been that this transporting and re-creating of religious acts online becomes a blending of features and information from multiple sources in ways that make spirituality online highly individualized and self-directed. Many who have studied religion online have argued that the very structure of the internet supports and even encourages the importing and combining of diverse religious activities. This is especially true for religious groups that seek to connect to religious sites, festivals, or fellow believers from which they might normally be disconnected because of time-space limitations.[23] Convergent religious practice online allows, and may even encourage, users to draw from traditional and new sources simultaneously. By importing religious practices online, believers have the opportunity to reexamine the context and application of various religious disciplines. This can promote experimentation that transforms some aspects of traditional religious practice in ways that challenge religious communities. No longer do you have to be an ordained minister to lead worship online. Creating liturgy online can mean adapting old rites and mixing in new forms of expression into a religious mash-up, as anyone can lead a Bible study or offer spiritual counsel in an online forum. Although modifying and mixing religious content and practice is not new—indeed, Christian missionaries have often adapted Christian practices and stories to local cultures—the ease with and speed at which this is now done is revolutionary.

The dynamic nature of network interactions and information online, which we have already discussed, often encourages a pic-'n'-mix approach, where people who have access to a wide range of options can blend different expressions of ritual and information from multiple sources to create self-directed forms of spiritual engagement online. The internet becomes for many a spiritual hub allowing believers to select from a vast array of resources and experiences with which they can personalize their religious behavior and belief. Instead of turning to recognized leaders for religious guidance, believers can use Google as a spiritual guide for accessing religious information and advice. However, religious users must use personal discernment to sort through the multitude of links provided, since Google's rankings of information are not impartial, the top recommendations being based on algorithmic rather than spiritual authority. Thus, searching and self-selection become important parts of spiritual seeking online.

Because the internet allows people to modify and perform religious ritual outside traditional structures, users often feel free to modify the customs and even the meanings attached to them. As a result, online convergent practice often represents a mixing of the sacred and the secular. One example of this is the variety of memorialization rituals that have emerged online allowing people to grieve and process tragedy in new ways, from virtual cemeteries allowing people to commemorate loved ones or pets, to web-based shrines that combine sacred and secular symbols or language. This is exemplified in the rise of tribute sites and memorial rituals emerging after the death of a celebrity, such as Michael Jackson in 2009. From the "Michael Mondays" that surfaced on Twitter, where fans tweeted memories about Jackson, to websites such as memories.michaeljackson.com, the internet provides a space for fans to create individual tributes and to communally grieve. Rituals commemorating death have always had religious links, and it can be argued that funerals and memorials in contemporary society have increasingly represented a mixing of religious and nonreligious symbols and elements. Not only do online spaces extend traditional death rituals to a wider, more public mourning community, but also memorialization becomes a public conversation and spectacle, so that online grieving offers participants a transcendent experience.[24] The online environment becomes an otherworldly space in which to connect with the deceased or use religious or mystical discourse to present preferred memories or sympathetic renderings of celebrities.[25] Thus, the internet encourages convergent practices by enabling individuals from diverse backgrounds and beliefs to come together and co-create activities and narratives that provide spiritual meaning for life events.

As the internet offers religious seekers a new degree of autonomy, and as more religious information becomes available online, the acquisition of religious knowledge becomes a highly individualized pursuit rather than one guided by traditional gatekeepers.[26] Individuals are encouraged to pursue religious knowledge that will benefit their personal lives rather than that which is prescribed by their community. This blending of practices and information from multiple sources by users may contribute to a self-directed form of spiritual engagement online. Removing established entry barriers, such as formalized mentoring or training requirements, may enable people online to bypass lengthy initiation processes traditionally required to achieve a place of religious prominence, though such roles are often contested or debated by offline religious authorities.

The flexibility of traditional practices and the tendency toward individualism online are not, however, limited to online religious practice. Researchers within other areas of internet studies have found that the internet may encourage a hyperautonomy, which we have described above in terms of networked individualism, a movement toward personalized networks facilitated by the social structures of network society.[27] As a result of this move from place-to-place to person-to-person connectivity, individuals switch more easily between social contexts and so have more control over what sources of knowledge they will draw on and what connections they will make. Some scholars have raised concerns about what effect this might have, especially on religious internet users. Armfield and Holbert found that because users primarily interact at an individual rather than a community level, this might encourage a "secularism model" even within religious engagement online.[28] Because the internet offers a marketplace of possibilities guiding users toward personalized convergent practices and individualized patterns of life online, the need to cultivate technology use in light of religious values becomes vital, especially for Christian communities.

Convergent practice shows how the internet becomes a toolbox for creating hybrids of traditional rituals that enhance personalized religious expression and individually oriented religious lifestyles. Such convergent practices have implications for expressions of communal faith.

Shifting Authority

The fluid nature of religious community and identity online has created a struggle between traditional religious leaders and what can be seen as a new breed of religious authorities appearing online. In response, in order to reestablish their positions of influence in a digital age, religious institutions are increasingly learning to leverage social media to build their influence and harness the power of the web to display their expert knowledge online. The result is that the internet is framed simultaneously as a threat to and a tool of empowerment for religious authority. This paradox is encapsulated by the notion of shifting authority. As new religious voices and experts emerge, religious institutions are forced to reexamine their previously established positions within a given community or institutional structure, responding to the new digital landscape.

For example, in February 2011 an American software company launched Confession: A Roman Catholic App designed to help users prepare for the Catholic sacrament of confession, an act normally administered by a priest. The app provided users with a list of questions to help them identify specific sins they had committed and would hence need to confess to a priest. While the creators consulted several Catholic religious leaders during the app's development, controversy ensued when a US bishop gave the app his imprimatur. This granted the app an official church license stating that it complied with Catholic Church doctrine and was thus acceptable for use within sacramental practices. This forced Vatican sources to respond, stressing that although the app was technically acceptable, it could in no way substitute for the embodied act of confession. The event echoed a decade-long standing tension between Catholic technology innovators and church officials regarding use of the internet for sacramental acts such as confession and prayer. It also highlighted how new media technologies raise questions of who or what determines the boundaries of acceptable religious practice in the internet age.

The internet is a place where renegotiations are occurring over who and what constitutes a legitimate religious leader and gatekeeper of knowledge. Through their design work, religious webmasters become mediators of religious institutional identity online. Forum moderators take on pastoral roles in the advice they offer members, and popular bloggers may be considered sources of expert religious knowledge by their loyal readers. As mentioned above, researchers have also noted the rise of "instant experts," as online prominence may allow people to influence others' perceived expertise online. Online experts are able to bypass time-honored religious training or prescribed initiation rites that would traditionally establish their positions offline. Online leadership roles have also been noted to influence individuals' standing in their offline religious communities. Herring's Christian newsgroup study showed how the roles established in online conversation communities, by introducing new forms of governing authority, may have the ability to inform and change perception of the power of offline religious hierarchies.[29] The internet thus allows online groups to transgress established religious structures by taking normally private discussions reserved for institutional administrators or leaders into public forums. This enables members to engage in debate on beliefs or policy often not possible offline. The rise in unofficial or unsanctioned sites for religious groups—such as websites offering spiritual counsel or the work of theoblogians who offer personal theological reflection and may have no formal training or background—illustrates the challenge that the internet poses to traditional, "legitimate" sources of theological knowledge.

While the internet challenges offline religious authorities, it can also provide opportunities for maintaining or reestablishing influence. Many churches and Christian organizations have recognized the need to be more deliberate and purposeful about their presence online; employing not only a webmaster but also a new-media director to manage an organization's social media presence is becoming more and more common. In line with this, many of the most influential religious bloggers and tweeters are those who also hold positions of religious leadership offline.[30] Increasingly, religious leaders offer teaching and guides about how online behavior should relate to established religious values and practices. Some communities even offer official policies or online filtering tools to help members discern what is considered acceptable internet usage that matches the values and priorities of their religious community.[31] The result is that the internet may be used to fortify community identity boundaries, creating another sphere to which religious groups must pay attention when they consider issues of religious education and discipleship.

Because the internet is framed as a threat to certain forms of authority by some and a tool of empowerment by others, it has become a sphere of negotiation between religious traditions and the values of network culture. We see a shift in priorities for what constitutes official and legitimate authority. In religious institutions and communities, authority has often been established by leaders' discernment of one's spiritual calling or divine selection or by one's undergoing religious training or rites of passage governed by set rituals. Authority is marked by prestige, position, and perceived power by others. However, in new-media culture authority may be constituted primarily on the basis of reputation systems (e.g., number of likes on Facebook, followers on Twitter, link rankings on blogs). It is the breadth of one's social network online that elevates one's voice and position online. This means that who is the legitimate voice for a particular community is changing in the internet age. Shifting authority raises important questions not only about how religious authority is now established and maintained in a digital society but also about what factors influence the position and place of religion in broader society.

Multisite Reality

When we look at the four characteristics described above—networked community, storied identities, convergent practices, and shifting authority—one area of overlap shines through. As the internet has become embedded in our everyday and spiritual practices, we see a clear integration of traditional or offline beliefs with online behaviors, and vice versa. The fifth characteristic of networked religion, multisite reality, describes the ways in which online practices are informed by wider beliefs as users integrate and seek to connect their online and offline patterns of life. There is an overlap between religious internet users and offline religious institutions. When we look closely at discussions of how the internet shapes sacred conceptions of time, space, and identity, we increasingly see a flow between traditional sources and structures of knowledge and their online counterparts.

A clear illustration of multisite reality is the way specific Christian practices online are commonly informed by wider Christian traditions. Christians online are frequently guided by the motivations or missions of the offline groups to which they belong. This means offline religious narratives and goals inform what they see as the purpose of the internet or how they justify their engagement with it. This has been especially true for Christian evangelicals with a strong call to missions and outreach and a long history of appropriating various media for evangelistic activities. From using the printing press for Bible distribution to using radio and television for evangelism or televangelism, evangelicals became some of the first religious internet users to see this technology through a distinctive lens. In the 1990s many evangelicals embraced the internet as a tool for making disciples by creating numerous books, online resources, and even organizations to help advocate and facilitate this central goal. Early initiatives like the Internet Evangelism Coalition (www.webevangelism.com) offered an online training course for would-be internet evangelists. Recognized organizations like the Billy Graham Evangelistic Association and the National Association of Evangelicals supported the emergence of Internet Evangelism Day (www.internetevangelismday.com), seeking to encourage Christians to embrace the internet as a tool to spread the Christian message.[32] Evangelicals have often framed the internet in prescriptive terms, arguing that the internet was divinely created to help fulfill their evangelical calling and Christian obligation.[33] Such arguments not only helped the group justify their use of the internet but also validated their wider mission and identity as evangelicals. Here recognized offline traditions and patterns of religious life directly framed and contextualized life online. This expression of multisite reality encourages the view that because the online environment is an extension of the offline religious social world, the internet should be infused with similar motivations and practices.

Increasingly, beliefs and behaviors from offline church traditions are imported into internet environments. In other words, online religious practice is intertwined with rather than divorced from traditional religious frameworks. Scholars noting the connection between religion online and offline have argued that, for many, online religious practice may simply be an extension of offline religiosity. For example, the internet allows immigrants in geographically dispersed contexts to connect with each other and their sacred homelands and create safe, supportive, and religiously tolerant environments.[34] For many, offline space and architecture serve as a template informing the design and function of churches.[35] For example, the architecture of an offline church may become the template for what churches should look like on a virtual-world platform, such as the Anglican Cathedral in Second Life being modeled after the York Minster, the Cathedral and Metropolitan Church of St. Peter in York, United Kingdom. Religious leaders often revert to historic narratives for a sense of orientation and to mark the internet as sacred space; thus, online use is informed by established religious narratives. Scholars have also found that religious groups' histories and beliefs inform their decisions regarding technology; similarly, these factors guide their choices related to how and why they use the internet.[36]

Because the internet has become increasingly assimilated into daily routines, researchers have recognized that patterns of internet use often arise out of users' offline patterns of behavior and beliefs.[37] Such findings challenge concerns that online practices might supplant engagement in offline groups or routines. Instead, internet-based social activities frequently serve as an extension or supplement to offline engagement[38] and in some cases may stimulate rather than reduce social interaction.[39] This contrasts with early pundits' claims that internet users would become "sad and lonely."[40]

Researchers recognize that the online-offline distinction has blurred as the internet has become embedded in everyday realities.[41] As Ess and Consalvo argue, the contradictory framing of the online versus the offline no longer holds true for many.[42] Yet this also means the internet represents a new space, a multisite reality, where aspects of online and offline culture become blended into a unique context that needs to be studied as a new actuality. Multisite reality highlights the fact that there are strong ties between individuals' online and offline attitudes, behaviors, and practices. Online routines become informed by offline ways of living, and a new cultural space emerges blending old and new values and expectations.

Implications of Networked Religion

Networked religion presents religious practice and culture online in terms of a network approach, where relationships, identities, and realities are shaped through loosely bounded affiliations established by individual user preferences and connection over traditional tightly bounded relations established through hierarchies. This creates a religious culture marked by a number of key characteristics. Through networked community we see that people online live simultaneously in multiple social networks that are emergent, varying in depth, fluid, and highly personalized. In storied identity we recognize that the religious self is malleable rather than fixed yet unified through connection to a shared religious narrative. Convergent practice shows that online religious rituals are often assembled from multiple sources in ways that build a self-directed form of spiritual engagement online. Shifting authority notes the paradox online as traditional religious power structures must adapt to and compete with new online gatekeepers and authority structures. Finally, the fact that networked religion represents a multisite reality suggests that the online world is consciously and unconsciously imprinted by internet users' offline values; thus there is a strong interconnection and potential movement between online and offline contexts, expectations, and behaviors.

In some respects, certain characteristics of networked religion, such as the drawing from multiple sources to create one's religious pattern of life or the seeking of a storied identity to live one's faith authentically, are not new. It can be argued that the internet is simply another resource people use in the ongoing process of negotiating the tension between the individual and the group, the expectations of tradition, and the benefits associated with personal preferences and freedoms. In this respect, religion has always been a negotiated practice. In this way, we see that religious practice online is connected to a social shift occurring within wider public performances of religion. By observing how traditional beliefs and relationships are renegotiated by individuals online, we see that networked religion illustrates just one arena in which the lifestyle trends within network society are impacting another (the religious) facet of contemporary society.

Besides speaking to the form of spirituality that emerges out of online networked negotiations with traditional religion, the concept of networked religion shows how current religious narratives, practices, and structures can become increasingly flexible, transitional, and transnational as they are lived out both online and in an information- and technology-driven society. It also provides a framework for us to consider how religion in a network society exists at the intersection between the online and offline worlds, between the digital and the embodied, and is informed by certain cultural values that encourage a certain view and practice of religion. This has foundational implications for Christians and their theological response to new media, which we will explore in the next chapter.

merging the network with theology

Who Is My Neighbor in Digital Culture?

Our exploration of technology, especially new digital media formats, in theology and media studies has highlighted a number of ethical concerns raised by new media. For instance, in chapter 2 we looked at how new media present us with the myth of interactivity. New media technologies offer users new levels of freedom to engage with people and information and new opportunities for creativity that can enhance spiritual practices and benefit Christian communities. Yet these same technologies can create spaces that encourage behaviors and practices challenging traditional norms and communication structures established by the technologies of print and electronic culture, especially related to issues of interpretation, authority, and community accountability in media use. Moreover, these new media spaces are not completely free but exist within sets of boundaries and behaviors defined and maintained by technological, commercial, and political constraints and power. This highlights the simultaneous opportunities and challenges new media technologies create for people of faith and their communities.

In previous chapters we have examined the nature of the networked environment, some of the ways in which Christianity has responded to developments in media and technology, and characteristics of networked religion. In this chapter we turn to what core issues or questions a Christian theology of the network might need to address in light of how new media technologies and spaces potentially shape the Christian life. The development of new digital media introduces some significant discussion topics for a faith whose symbols and imagery are typically rooted in physical everyday contexts such as agriculture.

For example, biblical passages in both the Hebrew Scriptures and the New Testament often draw on agriculture or nature to describe the relationship between God, human beings, and the wider world as well as the physical environment in which human relationships are realized. Common images include God as shepherd and humans as sheep, the kingdom of God as a mustard seed or a seed being sown, and nature imagery seen in the Psalms, all of which reinforce the physical dimension within the Christian faith. The emphasis on God becoming flesh and blood and living in the material world as Jesus of Nazareth (John 1), together with Scripture passages that talk about Jesus being present where two or three meet in person (Matt. 18:20), also reinforce that physicality. Thus, a faith that draws its analogies and metaphors from the physical environment—and a predominantly ancient, rural one at that—and that sees flesh-and-blood relationships as primary may struggle to find language to speak to virtual environments or even recognize the need to do so.

A networked theology must address questions relating to the relationship between the physical and digital worlds by considering what human identity, authentic human relationships, and community look like across those worlds. It must consider the ethical dimensions of how Christians can live wisely and wholesomely in a world that occupies both physical and digital spaces simultaneously. One way to begin thinking about these issues is to consider the idea of the neighbor, and by implication the neighborhood, in Jesus's teachings. This approach, which takes into account the essentiality of love of neighbor in Jesus's teaching about entering the kingdom of God, confronts us with the challenge of defining what that love of neighbor looks like in both the physical and digital worlds. In situating a networked theology around this frame—that our relationship to God is inherently linked to our relationship with others—we recognize three key questions that transcend our life in the physical world and have bearing on our digital interactions: who is my neighbor, where is my neighbor, and how should I treat my neighbor? The ways we respond to these questions, and the complex issues they raise, push us toward describing a theology of media and technology that bridges the gap between the physical and digital worlds.

Neighbors and neighborliness are familiar themes in Jesus's parables, such as the parable of the good Samaritan in Luke's Gospel (10:25–37). In this passage, a lawyer asks Jesus what is required for a person to inherit eternal life. Jesus replies with an answer echoing Deuteronomy (6:4–5) of loving God with all of your being and then adds the command to love your neighbor. Responding to the lawyer's query about who actually are our neighbors, Jesus answers with a story demonstrating who a neighbor is and how a good neighbor should act. We will return to this later in the chapter, but one thing important to highlight here is that the parable focuses on a certain person who needs assistance, placing us, the readers or hearers, simultaneously in the place of the injured one and the one who might act from a position of power.[1]

The connection between one's love for God and love for one's neighbor is echoed in other passages in the Gospels (e.g., Matt. 22:35–40; Mark 12:28–34) and seen in the Old Testament in Deuteronomy (6:4–5) and Leviticus (19:8). It also resonates with the prophet Micah's rhetorical question asking how we should live:

> He has told you, O mortal, what is good;
> and what does the LORD require of you
> but to do justice, and to love mercy,
> and to walk humbly with your God?
> (Mic. 6:8)

The very experience of living in the everyday world shapes questions of how God's people should live in right relationship with God and each other and also how they might seek to answer those questions faithfully. For the prophet Micah that response is influenced by the various practices of worship of the day and by the "lawsuit" God brings against the people of Judah (Mic. 6:1–8) for their behavior toward him and others. In Jesus's parables in Matthew (12:28–34), the everyday is framed in terms of what a true relationship looks like for those who see themselves as righteous before God and the stranger or neighbor with whom they do not share common ground. For us today, the questions "What may I do to inherit eternal life?" or "What does the Lord require of you?" have not changed, but the sociocultural context that shapes how those questions are asked and answered has. These questions become, "What does it mean to be the people of God in a technologized and media-saturated world?" or "What does the Lord require of you in our network society?" In the final chapter we will come back to Micah's call for justice, mercy (kindness), and humility in relation to neighborliness through our technological engagement. But first, in this chapter, we begin by considering who my neighbor is, where my neighbor is, and how I treat my neighbor in the multisite reality in which we live.

Who Is My Neighbor?

Our opening question relates to who our neighbor is in a digitally networked world. We have friends in social media, email and phone contacts, links to others' digital profiles through our online networks, and a wide range of other digital connections. Are any of these our neighbors in the theological sense? The biblical notion of the neighbor recognizes that the parties involved are subjects rather than objects. Thus, when reflecting on online friending, theologian Lynne Baab asks, "What are 'real' relationships in this new context? What are the characteristics of healthy, life-giving friendships in today's world? What choices and skills are necessary to navigate these new realities?"[2] Most important for our discussion is Baab's concern that we might consider hundreds or more people as friends or neighbors in our networked world but don't know the people who live in the house or apartment next door.

The Christian life is dominated by the theme of relationship in both individual and communal contexts. To be Christian is to be "in Christ" (e.g., Gal. 3:26–28). That short phrase, being "in Christ," has a range of meanings and connections, including being part of the community of Christ, the church; having faith in God through Christ and the Holy Spirit; and being united to Christ because he became human, lived, died, and rose again to both reconcile us to God through his mediation and demonstrate a new humanity saved from sin and broken relationships into partnership with God and others. As Daniel Migliore puts it, "To be Christian is to participate by faith, love, and hope in the new humanity present in Jesus, and that new humanity is one of renewed and realigned relationships."[3]

Furthermore, the Christian understanding of the nature of humanity is rooted in the idea that humans are at their core relational beings. This relates to the idea that human beings are made in the image and likeness of God (Gen. 1:26–28), which sees all humanity as somehow reflecting something of God, whether that be in human nature—for example, rational ability or moral capacity (e.g., Irenaeus, Augustine) or the capacity for social relationships with God and other people (e.g., Karl Barth, Emil Brunner)—or manifested as creative agency where humans represent God in the world and act as co-creators with God (e.g., Philip Hefner, Gerhard von Rad, David Clines).

Christianity is seen as an inherently relational faith in that it is based on the belief in the Trinity, that God is both three and one. The orthodox theological notion of the Trinity can be traced back to the fourth-century Cappadocian understandings of God and the attempt to describe God in a way that avoided both tritheism (three Gods) and modalism (one God revealed in three ways). Using the Greek terms "being" (*ousia*) and "reality" (*hypostasis*), Basil of Caesarea, Gregory of Nyssa, and Gregory of Nazianzu asserted that God has one *ousia* yet three *hypostases*, a formula affirmed at the Council of Constantinople (AD 381). In other words, God is three independent realities who share the same will, nature, and essence. This summary of the Trinity was further developed to highlight the internal life of God—the "immanent Trinity"—as a constant state of mutual interpenetration, partnership, purpose, dependence, and love. Therefore the three realities of God within the Trinity (Father, Son, and Holy Spirit) are understood to function in an unbroken fellowship of love with one another. This love, which is part of God's essential nature, declares and demonstrates for us that the core character of God is love, which shapes God's action toward the world. The "economic Trinity," God acting in the world, accords with God's eternal nature, and so God acts toward the world and those in it first and foremost in love.[4]

Christian reflection upon community often has been linked to this discussion of Trinity, as Christians are called by Christ to emulate this trinitarian relationality between one another and with the wider world. This is commonly expressed in how Christianity understands the nature of its own unique community, the church. By definition, a networked theology is inherently relational, with the network motif expressly describing various relationships within the network, and so we would expect to see manifested in it elements of this trinitarian relationality, together with understandings of community found in descriptions of the church, family, and neighborhood.

The Greek word for "church" in the New Testament, *ekklēsia*, is primarily linked to a formal assembly of citizens in a town, but it also contains elements of the Old Testament Hebrew word *qāhāl*, which reflects a process of gathering or the coming together of a community.[5] This provides a dual understanding of the church as both the local, gathered community in a particular time and place (e.g., 1 Cor. 1:2; 1 Thess. 1:1) and the community of all believers in Christ in all times and places (e.g., Eph. 1:22–23). The New Testament also speaks of Christian community as the people of God (2 Cor. 6:16; 2 Thess. 2:13–14), again reflecting the Old Testament concept of God creating and calling his people, and as the body of Christ (1 Cor. 12:27), emphasizing the church as the focal point of Christ's current activity (Col. 1:18). The church is also referred to as the temple of the Holy Spirit (1 Cor. 3:16–17; Eph. 2:21–22), reflecting the life imparted by the Spirit to the community of God. Therefore, in our construction of a networked theology within our digital and media worlds, aspects of community as the people of God, the body of Christ, and the temple of the Holy Spirit need to be present in some way.

Community is a dominant theme across the Hebrew Scriptures, as seen in the perspective that it is not good for humans to be alone and the corresponding creation of partners and helpers (Gen. 2:18); discussions of family that embrace extended families, clans, and nations; the covenants between God and human beings (e.g., with Abraham in Gen. 12–17 and Moses in Exod. 19–24); the cry for justice and righteousness in relationships (e.g., prophets such as Amos and Micah); and the intrinsic set of relationships between God, people, and the land.[6] These are all forms of relational networks with various feedback loops, configurations, and potential for both well-being and oppression. How might our networked theology critically take account of and reflect this multifaceted notion of community as well as its trinitarian and church-related dimensions? How should our networked theology reflect the primacy of love both of God and of our neighbor?

These facets of human and divine relationships, described primarily in terms of encounters in a physical environment, also stretch into our digital and virtual worlds and the boundaries between them and our physical worlds. For example, is flesh-and-blood presence, seen in the incarnation of God in Jesus of Nazareth and in physical church communities, a nonnegotiable in true Christian community? Are the notions of church limited to a completely physical representation in a particular time and place? Can one be truly human in an online environment, and how does one manifest love in that kind of environment?

Theological answers to these kinds of questions have typically drawn upon several core strands within the Christian tradition. First, human beings were intentionally created to be physical creatures, and rejection of this physical nature in favor of a spiritual or virtual world (as in gnosticism, for example) is to be resisted. Second, human beings were created to be social beings. Third, and perhaps most important, God became flesh and blood in the form of Jesus so as to provide a fuller revelation of God. Moreover, parts of Christianity require the physicality of sacraments (e.g., baptism, Holy Communion) as integral parts of their community identity. In some respects, these responses situate and ground the discussion of relationality and how to love God and neighbor within the limits of the physical world. As a result, discussions of religious community, friendship, and love in online contexts are often excluded from theological contexts, for they have not been considered part of true Christian community or life. This, in turn, puts the onus on the digital environments to justify their continuity with the historic Christian tradition to the wider church community. It is this challenge and opportunity that networked theology seeks to address.

The tension between online and offline communities can be seen in cases such as Life Church, which initially attempted to replicate the experience of attending church physically via internet and satellite technology but later moved to encouraging members to also participate in local groups for the purposes of discipleship, indicating that a fuller religious life might be found in a mix of online and physical relationships.[7] Going further, the Vatican states that religious experience online may be possible by the grace of God but that true community and the sacraments are present only in physical community.[8] However, many people see online churches as their primary community of faith, offering challenges to traditional institutions and their practices. This challenge has been recognized by reports such as the Church of England's 2004 *Mission-shaped Church*, which contends that the internet cannot be ignored when considering new forms of mission activity and church practice.[9] Taking up this challenge pushes the church toward what Christopher Helland categorizes as "online-religion," where the online environment generates further questions about the purpose and nature of the church, its authority structures, and what it means to participate in worship and community.[10]

The networked structure of the internet, and social networking in particular, as it relates to authority structures within the church typifies the frequent negotiations between trinitarian-based sentiments about physical community/church structures and church structures and those who see that relationality spilling over into the online networks and environments. For example, Dwight Friesen argues that pastors should become "network ecologists," seeing the church as a network of people and resources and building sustainable relational links between people both inside and outside their particular communities of faith.[11] Likewise, Kester Brewin argues that contemporary church life should be oriented around an adaptive network model that connects people, ideas, and knowledge with built-in feedback loops that allow that organization to learn and renew itself.[12] In contrast to more traditional top-down models, decentralized authority structures, he argues, will allow better information sharing and increased collaboration in theological tasks such as the interpretation of Scripture. One consequence of this, however, might be the shift that Susan White notes with this increased technological connectivity permeating the life of the church. Access to pastors and the meeting of spiritual needs become readily available and deliverable products, with an expectation of spiritual needs being met instantly and at any time of the day or night.[13] This connects to previous discussions of how digital culture encourages a sense of constant contact, where people develop unrealistic expectations for on-demand communication based on personal desires that can objectify social relationships.

The repositioning of authority and influence within the church challenges existing church structures and hierarchies that provide core identity and differentiation from other faith communities (e.g., Presbyterianism vs. Episcopalianism). Katharine Moody points out that this perceived antiauthoritarian streak might be seen in terms of socialization in the Christian community taking precedence over any conformance to a particular doctrinal structure or content.[14] Theology is done by all who draw upon their experience of Christian community and includes dialoguing with others outside established theological guilds and engaging the wider Christian tradition as desired. As blogger Tim Bednar puts it, "We are not convinced that pastors know more about following Christ than we do. We tire of having their vision delegated to us and instead are looking for the church to embrace our visions and dreams."[15]

The significance of these discussions about who can speak for a Christian community and who can be listened to should not be downplayed. The church, in its various forms, sees itself as a special community in relationship with God through Jesus Christ, possessing hope and good news for the world manifested by acting as God's agents in the world. The challenges to this community presented by media and communications technologies are met with both anxiety and anticipation, driving what Horsfield and Teusner identify as concrete examples of contextual theology—the dialogue between the past (represented by Scripture and tradition) and the personal or community experience engaged through the media.[16] Ultimately, what the church should be producing is an understanding sourced in both its theology and its experience.

The answer to the question of who is my neighbor connects directly to Horsfield and Teusner's call for a theology that understands and helps with living authentically, wisely, and justly in a digital world. The idea of being a neighbor implies a particular kind of relationship with another that produces well-being and nurtures life. Recognizing the other as a person or a subject rather than an object means we recognize their inherent worth, and this recognition is something we should strive for in all our relationships. Moreover, this recognition is reciprocal, for we also wish ourselves to be recognized as neighbors and hence persons of worth.

Twenty-odd years ago, Philip Meadows raised his concerns about the way in which digitally constructed worlds, such as the then-nascent virtual reality environments, might shape our perception of others and how this in turn would shape broader relationships between human beings and between humans and the natural world.[17] In particular, his anxiety was over how the boundaries between online and offline worlds might alter our perceptions of the physical world and our desire to be present in it, and to what extent the assumptions we make about things and people in either world are able to be carried over between worlds. For example, Meadows argues that Christians are called to be concerned with the transformation of this world and that a perception that an online life is more engaging or preferable to one in the physical world could generate an escapist mentality where the physical world is ignored and that transformative mission is lost. His question arising from this is how we, as Christians, can integrate our understanding of the different worlds we inhabit in such a way as to faithfully fulfill the call to follow Christ in every aspect of our lives.

That said, human beings are often caught between different worlds and cultures. Across history we have always had to learn how to negotiate with new cultural realities, working out to what extent forms of mediated communication are enough for genuine interaction and relationships between people. This negotiation occurs in the presence of migration, in cross-cultural mission, worship, and trade, in the face of globalization, and in learning a second language. The issue about what is lost if human beings never meet with others in person is not just restricted to the digital media age but arises whenever two people of different cultures meet in any aspect of life.

One way forward is to base our theology of the network on what makes us uniquely human and so capable of being a neighbor to another human being in both non-networked and networked contexts. Theologically, humanness is rooted first and foremost in God. There are biological, psychological, sociological, and cultural dimensions to being human, but the theological notion of true humanity is that human beings are bearers of the image and likeness of God. Biblically, this is seen in its fullness in the person of Jesus Christ, who is presented as the "image of the invisible God" (Col. 1:15) and represents what humanity's potential is in relationship with God, others, and the world. Understandings of human beings as God's image bearers tend to fall into one of three views. First, where the image is seen as intrinsically part of our human substance, typically connected to capacities such as rationality; second, where the image has a relational aspect allowing or present in relationship between God and human beings; and third, where the image is functional, manifested in humans representing God in the world through their agency. One helpful way of thinking about image bearing is a proposal by Latin American theologian José Miguez Bonino, which captures various aspects of these three interpretations.

For Bonino, the image of God in human beings comprises a number of interrelated aspects or dimensions that speak to human responsibility, agency, and relationality. First, image bearing conveys an aspect of freedom and responsibility upon the human person that allows him or her to choose to enter into genuine communion with God. This communion is expressed, Bonino contends, in responsible agency in the world, where human beings cultivate and care for the natural world and where the fullness of our humanity and image bearing is realized through loving others—God, human beings, and creation. Together, the combination of human-divine, human-human, and human-creation interactions makes up the image and likeness of God in human beings.[18] To be human is to be declared so by God, to be connected to relationship with God, and to be involved in loving agency in the world, wherever that might be.

Recognizing who is your neighbor is tied to recognizing another's value to God as a human being with his or her own relationship with God, also borne through image bearing. This understanding mirrors liberation theologian Gustavo Gutiérrez, who states that human persons are a sacrament of God, a medium through which God's grace is present in the world, in that each person represents God in the world. To act against another person is to act against God, and to act for another is to act for the Lord.[19] This sentiment is echoed in both the Old and the New Testaments (Gen. 9:6; James 3:9), which speak about how our actions toward other people are also toward the God whose image we all bear. We will pick up this theme of image bearing later in this chapter when we look at how we are called to act toward our neighbor.

Theologically, our humanity and community are sourced in God, and that remains the case whether in physical or digital environments. To be human is to be called to bear the image and likeness of God, who is, in essence, the trinitarian community of love, and then be called to bear that image in love of God and love of neighbor. The recognition of others as image bearers, as persons rather than things, and as neighbors is intimately connected with forming true community, which transcends purely physical environments. Thus, image bearing and being human are tied to agency in the world, whether digital or physical, reflecting the reality that those we encounter online are as much our neighbors as those over the backyard fence.

Where Is My Neighbor?

The question "Who is my neighbor?" leads us to ask, "Where is my neighbor?" If our neighbor is the one in whom we recognize true humanity rooted in the God whose image and likeness he or she bears, to what extent is neighborliness and this recognition of the other's true humanity rooted in a particular place and time? In the digital environment, can we have true neighborhood, and if so, what are the theological implications of this that in turn shape how we act toward those who might be our neighbors? In the following section we examine how the concept of neighborhood, as the place where we encounter God and other people and live our lives, expands beyond the physical and into digital environments. We propose that neighborhood overlaps the physical and that love of neighbor is imperative in both physical and digital environments.

We can approach the discussion of where my neighbor is by considering where and what neighborhood looks like in our current age. Considering the nature of neighborhoods is helpful for breaking down the barrier between physical and digital environments in order to see these spaces as continuums that we live in. In his short book *God Next Door: Spirituality and Mission in the Neighborhood*, Australian pastor and theologian Simon Carey Holt argues that the notion of neighborhood relates to our relationship with God and others.[20] For Holt, the three key dimensions that connect Christian faith and neighborhood are (1) neighborhood and human experience, (2) neighborhood and God, and (3) neighborhood and the church. Each is connected to a sense of place:

> The Christian story is a story of places—the most tangible places—from beginning to end. We are made to inhabit. Even the missionary who treks half way around the world does so to settle somewhere in particular and there to dwell for the sake of the gospel. The story of the incarnation is the story of God en-fleshed in a particular place at a particular time and within a very specific community. So too for us, the call of God is to be in a particular place and there to embody the presence and grace of God. It's a call to locality. Quite simply, it's a call to the neighborhood.[21]

Thus, neighborhood affects our existence as human beings, the way in which God is encountered, and how the identity and mission of individuals and the church are worked out in the everyday world.

Holt's first dimension is connected to an experience that gives us a clear sense of who we are in the world and where we belong. It is an experiential knowing that comes from being embedded in a particular location that bridges the gap between our private homes and the public worlds we find ourselves in. Of course, our notions of private home and public world begin to blur in a world where digital and physical environments overlap and permeate each other, which connects to some of the anxieties expressed earlier. Paradoxically, we can be in our private physical home yet present in a public online world. Our private conversations and presence exist within digital spaces while we are simultaneously in the public spaces of a workplace or rock concert or commuting on the train or bus. Thus, we live in that paradox of publicized privacy that we noted in an earlier chapter, where one can participate in the public digital world but, in doing so, now occupy a state of our private world that is continually connected to the public one.

The presence of physical or virtual boundaries often defines what we think of as public and private. This in turn can reshape our notion of neighborhood and even of home. Reflecting upon hospitality and homelessness, Brian Walsh and Steven Bouma-Prediger argue that in order for notions of hospitality and home to exist, and by implication the concept of neighborhood, established boundaries of some sort are essential.

> Without boundaries there can be no sense of "place" as home, as site of hospitality, security, and intimacy with local knowledge. Without boundaries there is no locality, and therefore no sense of membership in a particular community, family, or neighborhood which has an identity in distinction from other communities, families, and neighborhoods. Without boundaries identity is impossible.[22]

Therefore, part of the answer to the question of where is my neighbor is intrinsically linked to our understanding and perception of boundaries—not only where we see those boundaries existing but also how those boundaries came into existence, who those boundaries affect, and what happens when those boundaries are crossed. The biblical understanding of neighbor is most clearly seen in Jesus's parable of the good Samaritan (Luke 10:25–37), which encapsulates an inherent challenge to limited notions of neighborhood and human-constructed boundaries. Instead, the parable re-creates definitions of neighbor, neighborhood, and boundaries in light of a divine agenda that reflects the recognition of another's humanity sourced in God and independent of human criteria.

Elements of this parable are so well known that the term "good Samaritan" has entered into widespread usage to describe someone who helps a stranger in need. In response to the lawyer's question of who is the neighbor he is meant to love, Jesus's parable points to the neighbor who was an outsider but still showed love to the injured Jewish traveler. Moreover, the Samaritan's love is depicted as "engaging in all the powers of his personality: his sight, his heart, his hands, his strength, his time, his possessions, and his intelligence."[23] The key to the story, though, lies in the crossing or transgressing of existing boundaries within established social and cultural differences. This act—as the stranger follows the injunction to do justice, love mercy, and walk humbly with God—creates new boundaries and a new neighborhood. Thus, whether in the physical or digital world, our neighbors become those toward whom we act with justice, mercy, and humility, resulting in a relational rather than physical definition of neighborhood. As biblical scholar Christopher Marshall contends, "Love for neighbor cannot be separated from love for God. They constitute a single reality. Just as love for God must embrace all the dimensions of one's personality—heart, soul, mind, and strength—so too must one's love for others."[24] This has obvious implications for life in a hybrid of physical and digital worlds, and we have already noted in previous chapters that we have begun to see examples of spiritual practices being integrated across online and offline environments, whether by individuals or institutions. That said, this engagement with God and neighbor with all aspects of our being goes beyond just "religious" and "spiritual" practices and embraces all aspects of life in both online and offline worlds.

Holt's second dimension of neighborhood is that of neighborhood shaping our relationship with God. Our everyday life is the place where we wrestle with and live out our Christian faith. It is embedded in a particular time and place, and, increasingly, that place is nonphysical space. For Holt, "To pursue a placeless faith is to render theology impotent to address the real struggles of ordinary people in the here and now. For every struggle we face is one experienced in the daily places of life. In fact, those places themselves are also part of the struggle. That's certainly true of neighborhood."[25] Should we take Holt's critique seriously? If so, we will have to acknowledge that our theological reflection, both on our lives and generated by our lives, will need to take digital "places" into account.

Moreover, Holt argues that if we treat our everyday places, in his case the physical locations of life, as irrelevant to faith and spirit, we come to the point where we no longer think of God as present in those locations and thus remove any aspect of the sacred from them. In the case of digital places and the boundaries between the digital and the physical, this might also be the case, for if we see no place for God in our online activity and life, so too the online world loses its capacity as a site for the sacred and encounters with God. In part, this might occur because, while Christianity has significant symbolism and imagery to describe human-human and human-divine relationships, these tend to be seen primarily through agricultural or political images with a physical connection (e.g., lost sheep, heavenly city, mountain of the Lord, tree of life). Some, such as sociologist Brenda Brasher, argue that Christianity has yet to develop, or choose to develop, the appropriate symbols and religious imagination to engage with digital spaces.[26] Others, such as technologist Kevin Kelly, however, would argue that technology, and by implication the digital world, might be a better mirror of God than is the natural world, for technology forces us to confront new creative spaces and human agency that have God-like qualities.[27] We believe networked theology will help address some of these critiques and opportunities.

The focus on the natural world is understandable, because Christianity sees the history of our world as one that starts and ends with God's interaction with the natural world and with God's activity within that world. While God is not part of the world, as in pantheism and some panentheist worldviews, neither is the creator God absent from the world, as in deism. God is not dependent upon the created universe, though God can be encountered in the physical world and sees it as of great value (Gen. 1:31; John 3:16; Col. 1:15–23). Whether it be the places in the Old Testament where individuals or communities encountered God or the stories of places and encounters in New Testament books such as the Acts of the Apostles, God is encountered in physical places. The Christian understanding of the incarnation, that God became flesh and blood in the person of Jesus Christ, manifesting both full humanity and full divinity, reinforces the significance of the physical. Incarnational theology, though, moves beyond just a physical encounter with God in Jesus and, as Holt puts it, has "its impact upon every aspect of life, from our daily work to the food we eat, from the places we choose to inhabit to the relationships that color our lives. God is a God of place."[28] Therefore, if our world now includes new nonphysical places and representations of human life, we should not be surprised to find God, who is Lord of all, present in our digital spaces and our human encounters there.

This leads into Holt's third dimension of neighborhood, the interaction between church and neighborhood. The first two dimensions speak to the everyday worlds we find ourselves in as the places that generate our sense of personal identity as human beings. This is a starting point for our thinking about the God we encounter in the world. The third dimension extends the notion of neighborhood to include ethical and communal aspects of how the people of God, the followers of Jesus Christ, live out their lives faithfully in those everyday worlds. Jesus's teaching and ministry speak to the interplay between faith and agency in the everyday world. This is seen in the call to love God, neighbors, and enemies, in the commands to proclaim the good news of the kingdom of God, and in the recognition that this world, and all that is in it, matters to God.

All of this brings the concept of neighborhood and the location of human activity into focus. Holt states that we are all part of an "embedded community," where we are found, are shaped by, and encounter each other, and exist within particular neighborhoods. If we exist in both physical and digital worlds, which often overlap in interesting and novel ways, the neighborhood in which we are embedded spans those worlds too. Or perhaps we are present in more than one neighborhood. Moreover, as with any neighborhood, the more we know about it and the people in it, and the more we participate in it, the better we know and are known by those in it.

This identification of neighborhood as being spread across physical and digital environments highlights several critical challenges. The first is that the digital environment is not going to go away in the foreseeable future. Rather, with the proliferation of augmented reality, mobile media, and internet, it promises to grow and become interconnected with our physical environment and to give rise to distinct digital places or neighborhoods for people. Adapting Holt's line of thought, the digital environment becomes a neighborhood in which we will find, in some way, our sense of identity, an encounter with God, a location for personal and communal reflection, and a place where we are called to faithfully live and love our neighbors. That last part brings us to our third question in this chapter, how should I treat my neighbor in a digital world?

How Should I Treat My Neighbor?

The previous sections have highlighted the fact that who our neighbor is in a digital world is determined not by human perception but by humanity rooted in God's determination. We have also argued that digital spaces, in conjunction with the physical world, form a continuity with our everyday neighborhoods. In fact, the continuum or bridging of digital and physical spaces often forms the places where we experience our valued social interaction and even encounter God. This is the space where the people of God are called to be. Given this, how might a networked theology talk about how we are to engage with those who are our neighbors in these hybrid spaces, where the physical and digital aspects of everyday life meet?

As we saw above, the concept of neighbor in the parable of the good Samaritan is tied to the reality that love for our neighbor cannot be separated from our love for God. This is a love for God that matches God's determination of humanness and what that might look like in its fullest. It means taking seriously the fact that the love of God is genuinely realized in an activity of love and justice in the everyday world, addressing the abuse of power (Amos 3:13–5:24), care for the poor and oppressed (Matt. 25:31–46), and the integrity of faith and works (James 2:14–26). In effect, love of neighbor is worked out through a combination of orthodoxy (right belief), orthopraxy (right action), and orthopathy (right feeling). It engages the whole person relationally, as the whole person is engaged in loving God.

Christian sociologist David Lyon asks whether being "wrapped in media" adds or detracts from the human capacity for relationships.[29] In one sense, it extends the abilities of human beings to network and communicate with others in new and powerful ways, but it may remove a level of meaning from that interaction, making communication dependent upon voluntary self-disclosure brought about by relationships of trust that are harder to sustain. Lyon does not deny the power of digital technologies to facilitate communication but states that the use of digital technologies requires care and control at both personal and corporate levels (e.g., surveillance). For him, the virtues of love and trust must guide this, a concern echoed by the Vatican, which sees the fundamental guiding principle for the use of media of social communications to be "by persons to persons for the integral development of persons."[30] Lyon asks the simple question, "Would God use email?" (which could be expanded to include any digital communication technology) and comes to the conclusion that God uses the technology through the disciples of Christ but that he uses it circumspectly.

This spills over into theological discussions about the nature of personhood, community, and human relationships with each other and the wider world. At its most pragmatic level, grassroots theological reflection is often tied to the welfare and practice of the Christian community and how digital technologies might threaten that. At one level, this concern is produced by a digital environment that prioritizes individualized control, an aspect of media culture we noted in chapter 2 as promoting individuals rather than communities as shapers of social boundaries and adopters of technology for personal mediated communication. This raises anxieties within communities that result in books and articles being published about keeping young people safe on the internet, internet pornography and pastoral ministry, and how a church's use of the internet needs to align with its faith commitments.[31]

Discussions relating to being wrapped in media, current practices of Christian communities, or how individuals should live tend to address the neighbor in the traditional sense of physical human beings. Yet we also need to focus on issues of identity, intent, experience, and effects on individuals and communities posed in the nonphysical, digital worlds. For example, as online worlds became more prevalent, questions about how virtual entities should be treated in those worlds began to surface in theological deliberations.[32] Similarly, questions about ethics being "a function of our experience or reality" concern Graham Houston in his consideration of whether the online world creates the true postmodern world of ethical relativism, where individuals can be free of moral responsibility to God and fellow humans.[33] Both Houston and Meadows would reject the possibility that there are godless places, with Meadows arguing that a Christian understanding of God rejects that there are places able to be created that are "private" from God. Houston goes further, developing what he calls a "virtual morality" that draws from a moral order based on the created order, freedom in Christ resisting technological determinism, and normative principles derived from divine love. In this scheme, Houston argues that a participant's subjective experience in the online environment is primary and ethical guidance principally engaging with the intention and desire of the participant and the effects of those intentions is secondary. Moreover, Houston offers this scheme not just to Christian believers for application in their personal lives but also to the wider public, arguing that in a pluralistic society his theologizing can enter into the wider ethical conversation about digital technologies.

A networked theology such as Houston's thus advances into the public sphere, reflecting not only individual matters but also a concern about societal structures and processes. It declares that theology has something constructive to contribute to wider societal engagement with technology and media. For example, Eric Stoddart argues that the contemporary practice of surveillance and its increasing significance in internet societies can be addressed through the theme of truthful speech rooted in the biblical tradition.[34] In particular, he argues that the relational responsibility to the other and the critical examination of the role of centralized control of surveillance are essential to maintaining human dignity in a society increasingly under digital surveillance. A networked theology should seek to address these kinds of issues constructively as much as it seeks to shape communities of faith and the individual Christian life.

Theological engagement also targets a range of wider issues related to digital technologies, from the perception that digital technologies generate an unhealthy emphasis on "cyber-libertarianism" to information poverty and the marginalization of individuals and communities in an increasingly digital world.[35] Whether it be a Roman Catholic understanding of social concern stemming from human dignity and the call for the faithful transformation of all aspects of the world or a Protestant one linked particularly to biblical injunctions to be just and compassionate, Christianity brings these frameworks into its reflections on digital technologies. In particular, "digital divides," the possibility of persons being objectified and digital technologies becoming an end in themselves rather than a means to an end, are concerns theology seeks to investigate and comment critically on in the public sphere.[36] These challenges, whether for individuals, the Christian church, or wider communities, call for a recognition of neighbors and neighborhood that demands a radical acknowledgment of the humanity present in those we encounter in both physical and virtual worlds. This perspective also refuses to remove the presence of God from those virtual neighborhoods and encourages us to treat our physical and virtual neighbors with a love and justice that goes beyond the individual.

The Rise of a Networked Theology

Knowing who our neighbors are, where they are located, and how we should act toward them lies at the heart of a networked theology. Networked theology takes seriously the belief that God's involvement with human beings is not limited to the purely physical, everyday world but is also active in the digital locations we create and inhabit. It requires that we treat individuals and communities as subjects and persons, not objects and things; it sees our relationship with God in Christ as integral to how we live and treat others in a world where the digital and physical overlap each day. Moreover, it calls us to take seriously some of the very real identity issues that arise out of the digital technology and media being created and to think imaginatively about how we engage with those issues faithfully, lovingly, and justly. We will revisit these issues in chapter 6 as we explore what a theologically based, appropriate technology that stands in continuity with Christianity's past, present, and future might look like.

5

developing a faith-based community response to new media

This chapter maps out a framework for reflecting on and moving toward a communal response to new media. It presents a four-layer strategy to help religious groups think through and develop a theologically informed response to digital media. This strategy is adapted from a religious-social shaping approach to technology, which was originally developed to help scholars study how and why religious communities make the choices they do regarding new media use.[1] This approach emphasizes the fact that, when deciding how they will engage technology, religious groups often prioritize communal and spiritual values above technological affordances or advantages. Here it is translated into a reflective framework guided by a set of questions to help religious individuals and groups reflect on how their media use does or should relate to their community's beliefs and mission.

The religious-social shaping approach to technology grew out of more than a decade and a half of study on how different religious groups respond to new media and online cultures. It was initially presented in the book *When Religion Meets New Media*.[2] We argue that this approach not only is of use to scholars who study media but also offers a blueprint that faith communities can use to actively reflect on their technology use in light of their religious beliefs. It is presented here to help groups and individuals carefully consider how new media may need to be adapted or "cultured" so that they fit within their core convictions and key practices. The aim of this chapter is not simply to offer an intellectual exercise that provides a sociological explanation for how religious groups interact with new technologies, or to offer a list of explicit steps providing a one-size-fits-all theology of new media. Rather, this chapter outlines a clear process and resources Christians can use to better understand the impact of digital technology on our spiritual lives and consider how technology use and trends may affect the church in the future.

Responses to Media

To begin this journey, we must consider how and why Christian groups respond to technologies in particular ways. When we look at the motivations behind religious communities' choices about technology, we see that reactions to media typically fall along a continuum of response. John Ferre, a scholar of media and religion, argues that religious groups typically take one of three stances, seeing media as a conduit, a mode of knowing, or a social institution.[3] These responses closely echo Barbour's typology of response to technology—optimism, pessimism, and ambiguity—outlined in chapter 2. Yet Ferre's continuum is discussed here because it specifically highlights certain praises, critiques, and justifications given by religious groups regarding their beliefs about the impact and implications of media technology on their communities.

Media as a Conduit

According to Ferre, some groups view media as a conduit. A conduit is a pipeline delivering whatever is placed in it from point A to point B. Here media are seen as simple delivery systems transporting content from the media producer to the consumer. What is important is the message that the media technology is transporting, rather than the technology itself. Media are seen as neutral, as functional tools that simply relay the values of the content they carry. When media technology is perceived in these instrumentalist terms, it allows religious groups to have a positive response to media. In fact, media are easily described as gifts from God, tools given by God for relaying spiritual messages to our chosen audience. Clearly, the media-as-conduit approach echoes technological optimism, presenting media in a positive light. It emphasizes how technology can make the world a better place for the faithful, and it encourages people to embrace media technology because it offers great potential for innovation and for getting religious messages out or accomplishing religious goals. This response can be readily seen in some groups' appropriation of technologies for evangelism. These groups have argued that media technologies, from the printing press to the internet, offer the potential to reach a mass audience, and because the content determines the nature of the technology, media can and must be embraced to accomplish the Great Commission. Indeed, this argument has been used to frame and promote the internet as a vital field for mission work.[4]

Media as a Mode of Knowing

Other groups assert, often in response to those who promote a neutral view of technology, that media instead are value-laden artifacts or environments. Ferre describes this as seeing media as a mode of knowing, evoking the idea that technology has its own built-in logic and value system. This perspective is often linked to the work of Jacques Ellul, who argued that human society has become dominated by "*technique*" or science and that the scientific system's chief values of progress and efficiency have created a value system that promotes a dependence on technology.[5] Sometimes this perspective has been referred to as technological determinism, as the nature of technology itself is seen to determine its outcomes and impacts.

Many taking this perspective, which mirrors technological pessimism, argue that values of media technology are antithetical to religious values. For instance, Christian scholars who were concerned about the impact of television on society in the 1980s evinced this perspective, arguing it was an entertainment medium that discouraged critical thinking and promoted anti-Christian values.[6] If that is the case, if media promote problematic morals and spiritual values, we need to be cautious of technology. This view frames media as all-powerful and seductive. Thus, media users must discern the value system that the media are promoting, because our engagement with media will inevitably lead us toward those beliefs. Christian communities adopting this perspective have often had a very negative, or at least a very cautious, view of media and are suspicious of its use. To what extent can we truly use the internet for sharing religious purposes? Will it co-opt our mission and subvert our theology? Quentin Schultze warns that the internet promotes a technologized culture that works against Christian values of community, truthfulness, and reciprocity.[7] This perspective encourages religious users to be suspicious of media, lest they cultivate or unknowingly promote values that run counter to their faith through their interaction with the media.

Media as a Social Institution

In many respects both of the above perspectives are valid. They represent two ends of a continuum, with media as a conduit or a completely neutral technology on one end and media as a mode of knowing or a seductive, value-laden technology on the other. Therefore, it is important to consider a middle ground. This hearkens back to our previous discussion of technological ambiguity, where technology is viewed as value-neutral, though susceptible to the positive or negative intentions of its users. Ferre describes this in another way, seeing media as a social institution. Here emphasis is placed on the fact that media may have certain embedded values because of designers' intentions or their most common uses. These values can influence users toward certain behaviors and ways of thinking. Yet media technology is also a tool that can be shaped both by those who create it and by those who use it. Media as a social institution focuses our attention on media systems of production as well as users' reception of their form and content. Here, both "content and technology matter, but neither is determinative."[8]

This approach highlights the fact that media do not emerge in a vacuum. Instead this realm is a people-centered enterprise, created by people who are motivated by distinct goals or outcomes and used by people who may have alternative desires and intentions. This approach requires careful discernment. The outcomes of media use are not inevitable; rather, they are dependent on the context, the process of appropriation, and people involved in the media's use. Here the internet is seen as a social as well as technological system. Internet use is informed by the people who use it—their motivation and specific values connected to the culture that it promotes. This means that while a technology may be designed for one purpose, thus encouraging certain beliefs and behaviors tied to that intention, it is often appropriated for different purposes. For instance, the internet was created by the US military complex as a secure communication system that would protect the US government from the threat of nuclear war. However, when people use Facebook or email, it is typically not with the intent to aid or support the defense industry. Over time, the networking capabilities offered by the early internet were noted by its users as an important feature of the system. The ability to communicate with people across time and space could be used not only to exchange research ideas but also to discuss personal interests, from programming hacks to science fiction to religion. The internet became more than a research tool; it became a space facilitating social interaction.

With this understanding, religious groups need not shy away from media, because they can purposely shape technology for their goals and present media content in light of their beliefs. However, they must critically reflect on how the nature of media technology may impact their communities. This requires religious communities to be both technologically savvy and able to discern the long-range implications of their choices.

Religious Communities and Reflection on Technology

Over the past fifteen years researchers like us have focused much attention on understanding how and why different religious communities and organizations have responded to new media technologies in particular ways. Some of this attention has been focused on the roots of the religious-social shaping of technology, which began as a comparative research study of how various Christian, Jewish, and Muslim communities negotiate new technologies in light of their religious and cultural values.[9] This research included looking at the ways modern Islamic groups in Turkey justified their appropriation of television and web platforms to spread their religious beliefs, how members of the emerging church movement in the United Kingdom and the United States have leveraged blogs to build support networks to solidify their religious identities, and even at the ways Israeli ultra-Orthodox Jews and rabbinical leaders have attempted to adapt the cell phone into a "kosher" technology, supporting community needs and boundaries. Fifteen case studies of the different strategies were analyzed by Heidi Campbell to see whether any common patterns existed in the ways these groups used and responded to new media. For instance, was there something different between, say, Christian and Muslim responses to the internet, or were there similarities?

The study revealed that it was not so much the religious tradition that dictated the particular response to technology (e.g., an overarching Christian or Jewish response to technology) but, rather, it was a group's goals, mission, and core values that guided its response to technology. No matter the religious tradition, each community, in one way or another, evaluated the benefits and challenges offered by the technologies it chose to engage through a religiously informed decision-making process, even if that process was not always articulated at an official level by recognized religious leaders. Whether it was Muslims in Turkey considering how to integrate new media resources to spread their beliefs to a wider audience or Exclusive Brethren in New Zealand seeking to create a closed computer and internet system so its use did not violate the social boundaries of their group, all of the groups made deliberate choices about how and why they used or avoided a particular technology, choices in line with their core religious values, priorities, and utilitarian motivations. Evangelicals in the United States using the internet for evangelism had much in common with Orthodox Jews in Israel using the web as a way to call secular Jews back to a religious lifestyle. Both groups shared a motivation to use technology for outreach and so structured their use of the internet and work online to facilitate that primary goal. Both spoke about the internet as an asset to their mission and as a divine resource for accomplishing these purposes.

When considering the source of a religious community's technological choices, it becomes important to trace the patterns of thought and logic that influence the ways that the community talks about technology. Through this research it became clear that faith-based groups undergo belief-based negotiation in relation to their technological choices. In fact, in many cases they share similar motivations. While the religious-social shaping approach to technology grew out of a more theoretical reflection to help describe different religious groups' responses to media, it also provides groups with tools they can use to reflect on their own responses. This approach takes Ferre's stance of seeing media as a social institution in which people, especially members of religious communities, play an important role in shaping the outcomes and implications of technologies.

Social Shaping of Technology

Our thinking in this chapter has also been informed by the theory of the social shaping of technology that comes from science and technology studies (STS). The basic argument made within this theory is that it is essential to examine a group's social processes when considering how the group is influenced by a given technology and how it chooses to respond. This means not only focusing on the technology but also looking at the users, the designers, and how both make choices and talk about technology. This theoretical framework emerged as a response to technological determinism, which scholars saw as being overly focused on technology as an all-powerful force and not giving enough attention to the choices that users make and how these impact technology use.

Scholars such as Roger Silverstone, Eric Hirsch, and David Morley developed this alternative perspective to study how families domesticate technologies to fit in the framework of a given family.[10] One of their key assertions was that, when it comes to technology choices, families are not only governed by economic constraints but also guided by moral and value boundaries. The scholars called this value centeredness, or a moral economy, which constrains and dictates the way families adopt, use, or even manipulate technologies to meet the needs and boundaries of their value systems. Think about how and why parents set limits on the amount of television their children are permitted to watch; their justification is often grounded in certain beliefs about the technology and how it influences their children's behavior and family life. We suggest religious communities function in very similar ways to families, meaning that their systems shape their technologies. By looking at religious communities as a family of users with a distinctive moral economy, we see how they make choices about technology, how they talk about these decisions, and how those choices are affected.

Diane Zimmerman Umble used this approach to reflect on the Amish response to the telephone.[11] She found that this closed community responded to this technology with resistance and reconstruction. Amish communities function as a tightly woven family with a morally grounded response to technology. They resist any technology that proves problematic for the ethical and social boundaries of the community, especially key values such as the call for members to be separate from the secular world, be humble, resist vanity and the exultation of the self, protect the sanctity of the home and family, and live as pacifists. The telephone initially was banned in Pennsylvania Amish communities because of the perception that it violated core values such as humility and separation from the outside world. Yet if you visit some Amish communities in Pennsylvania today, you will see a structure that looks like an outhouse at the intersection of several farms. This is actually a telephone booth that houses a shared phone for multiple families. Wireless and cell phones are used but typically kept at places of business rather than in the home, as they are seen as communal resources, not an individually owned technology. So the telephone was taken out of the home to prevent disruptions to the Amish social order. The community resisted the way the phone put individual communication before the family and reconstructed the phone's presence in the community in line with the moral economy of the community. This research offers some important guides for developing a Christian response to technology. We suggest combining the reflection on the values and processes ingrained within religious communities with a social-shaping-of-technology lens that focuses on how user communities negotiate with technology.

Religious-Social Shaping of Technology

From the above observations, we note that religious groups typically (consciously or subconsciously) undergo a four-stage process regarding their choices about technology. These include the following:

1. *History*—the history and tradition of the community that shapes who they are and what they stand for;
2. *Core Beliefs*—core beliefs of the group that relate to their general beliefs and choices related to media;
3. *Media Negotiation*—the negotiation and decision-making processes they undergo, as it relates to a new technology grounded in the first two areas; and finally

4. *Community Discourse about Technology*—the communal framing and discourses created by a group to justify their technology use in light of their values and identity.

While these four stages were initially developed as a method for scholars wanting to study how religious groups negotiate their technology use, they also provide a helpful framework that religious groups can use to reflect on their beliefs about media and move toward developing a theologically informed reflection on new media. A key premise underlying what is described as the "religious-social shaping of technology"[12] is that religious communities often do not reject new forms of technology outright but rather undergo a process of evaluation and dialogue to determine what effects new technology may have on the beliefs or behaviors dictated by the communities' values. If the technology encourages behaviors or beliefs that run counter to the ethos of a community, a decision must be made about whether the technology must be resisted altogether or, more likely, what specific uses or aspects of the technology must be resisted or reconstructed if the technology is to be used. This process may even lead to innovation, where technical aspects or structures are modified to fit with the community's social and religious life.

Often scholars begin by looking at the media negotiation process of a given group rather than beginning with the important backdrop that contextualizes these choices. We would argue that in order to understand religious communities' use of new media, it is important to consider the four core layers of reflection listed above. In the following sections, we will look at how this method can be applied to a Christian group's reflection on media choice, providing a template for reflection on personal and communal motivations behind media usage. This is not an easy task. Members of a given community have vested interests, and it can be difficult for an insider to take on the objective, evaluative position of the outsider that is often necessary when doing this type of deep reflection. As suggested in chapter 1, building a theological response to technology involves engaging both instrumental and cultural reflection on media. This means stepping back and identifying the cultural structures, relationships, meanings, and values at work within a given context or community and looking at how decision making regarding media is informed and can be linked to these. To help readers engage in this type of reflection, this chapter seeks to carefully spell out and provide examples of the four layers of analysis offered by this approach. It then offers concrete questions that can be used by individuals and groups seeking to go through a similar process of discernment. By looking at each of these four areas, we will see how, taken together, they offer a systematic platform for critical self-examination of how religious values can and should connect with technological choices.

History: Uncovering the History and Backstory of Technology Appropriation

The first layer of reflection is to consider the history and tradition of a given Christian group. A community's position toward and use of different media do not emerge in a vacuum but arise over time, shaped by decisions or events from that community's history. If someone really wants to understand why their community makes the choices that it does, they need to look at the background of the group. Where is it coming from? What is its theology? What events or experiences in the past have defined its character and identity? Each of these questions helps reveal who the group is as a community and how it defines itself as a cohesive and unique body. Related to the background, it is important to identify the authority structures of the group and how these relate to its tradition. Religious structures and leaders often offer advice or set guidelines related to what is considered the way of life for a given group. Uncovering how a specific group responded to the printed word as an early form of media can also be useful, since many religious groups enacted the same pro/con, threat/asset arguments regarding the rise of the printing press as they do regarding each new form of media that arises. Decisions made regarding texts, one of the earliest forms of media, thus serve as a template for future negotiation with other media. It is crucial to look at these background issues to see where the group's values and beliefs emerge from, because those values and beliefs shape its responses to media.

In order for an individual or group to uncover the key background elements that create the values platform guiding the community's response to technology, it is vital to reflect on the Christian tradition to which it belongs or connects. Understanding how the community defines itself and sees its roots informing its communal identity becomes important, because this is the ground from which the group's values emerge. Different denominations may vary in their expectations of community membership, authority structure, liturgy, and worship. Different churches will have nuanced understandings of what constitutes Christian community and practice and who can make the decisions defining these. For example, within Presbyterian and some Reformed churches, authority is based at the local level on an assembly of elders elected by members of the local congregation, where the pastor serves as a "teaching elder" but is part of this general governing group of the church. Other denominations, such as the Episcopal or Lutheran churches, are more hierarchically structured. They are governed by a bishop who oversees the clergy of churches in a given region and by annual synods or council meetings where local churches elect individuals to represent their church's interests. The authority structure of a given church or faith community is important because it determines who is responsible for making choices impacting church practices and policies, which can relate to issues of technological decision making. Even groups within the same tradition may differ on these issues, as seen in American Baptist versus Southern Baptist versus British Baptist understandings of church life and practice. Even newer Christian movements unaffiliated with a larger denominational tradition have a history that defines what constitutes group membership, authority, and view of scriptural texts, all of which undergird responses to media. Therefore, self-reflection on what section of the Christian tradition one affiliates with is important for understanding how this might direct or provide resources for one's response to technology.

The following questions are a starting point for reflecting on how the Christian tradition may inform a community's technological decision making:

- How does your faith tradition/affiliation shape your Christian identity and define your mission?
- How does your group define itself as a community?
- What is its authority structure, and how does this guide or determine communal decision making, especially related to media?
- What has been the group's relationship with text and mass media?

Reflecting on these questions can help individuals and groups identify what teachings or beliefs have guided the group's previous choices and reactions to media. Communal decision making regarding technology does not exist within a vacuum; the responses emerge over time. Therefore, it is essential to uncover and reflect on decisions or events in the community's history that might have shaped these decisions.

Core Beliefs: How Religious Community Values (Should) Inform Media Values

After one has gained a good sense of the background of a given group—understanding how it defines itself, its structure, and how it seeks to present itself in the world—a second level of reflection begins. Here the dominant or core social values of the group, which often inform technological decision making, are identified. In the case of the Amish discussed above, core values such as the sanctity of the home/family and humility influenced the group's critique and restructuring of the use of the telephone. Those using the religious-social shaping of technology approach must investigate the core beliefs and patterns of a community to see how these are lived out and shape the behavioral expectations of the group in light of faith. Because a group's values and priorities may change over time, it is important to recognize the context of the group—that is, the culture and historical moment in which it finds itself. For instance, evangelical Christians in Seattle, Washington, may have different priorities relative to how their faith should be lived out and explained in their culture than evangelicals in Atlanta, Georgia, do in theirs. The way Lutherans in Minnesota negotiate their faith in contemporary life differs in nuanced ways from Lutherans in Germany as a result of the social, cultural, and political climate in which they find themselves.

This can be seen more concretely in the difference between Presbyterians in New Zealand and the Presbyterian Church in Scotland, where Presbyterianism arguably originated. The Church of Scotland, which is the Scottish manifestation of Presbyterianism, emerged out of the Protestant Reformation and the work of reformer John Knox, who sought to transform Christian practice in light of problems he saw inherent in the Catholic Church structure and worship practices of his time. As such, Scottish Presbyterians are steeped in and connected to the historical roots and theological convictions that emerged from the formation of the tradition in the eighteenth century. The Presbyterian Church in New Zealand has a very different history, being planted by Scottish settlers who came to the country in the mid-nineteenth century. Being in New Zealand, a much younger country and geographically far removed from the historical center of the tradition, the church is situated in a more secular culture and has less influence, since it is not a state church as it is in Scotland. Such factors strongly influence the group's identity and how it approaches reform principles and its role in the greater culture. While Presbyterian churches in both Scotland and New Zealand hold similar doctrinal beliefs about the role and importance of Scripture, it can be argued that there is greater flexibility in the New Zealand context, which, because of its distance from the source (Scotland), allows for more innovation within local church contexts and skepticism toward the tradition within national-level decision making. For instance, since 2011 the New Zealand Presbyterian Church has run a cell phone and Facebook project during Passion week (the week leading up to Easter). The public is encouraged to sign up for daily messages offering an unfolding of the Easter story written as first-hand news updates from various biblical characters. This informal and often playful reporting has received a lot of press as a creative way to engage the wider public rather than primarily members in the story behind the Easter season. Because the New Zealand Presbyterian Church is a minority denomination, it focuses much of its media work on outreach and seeks to uniquely engage the cultural and nonreligious context in which it finds itself. This confirms the fact that identifying the cultural context and agenda of a specific group at a particular given moment is essential, as those core values and how the group seeks to present itself in society shape its interaction with technology. Core values derived from a historically grounded tradition must always be contextualized and applied anew to the social, cultural, and historical context in which a given community exists.

With this in mind, individuals and groups seeking to reflect theologically on technology need to pay close attention to how beliefs can and should guide decision-making processes related to media use. Identifying a group's core theological beliefs that set them apart, as well as its distinctive religious identity and missional priorities, offers members an agenda for interaction with other members and contemporary culture. The values that define a given group can easily determine how it chooses to approach media so that it supports the identity and structure of the community. If a particular religious community focuses its mission on issues of social justice and the service of the poor, then it would make sense that such a group would adopt or adapt digital technologies to serve such goals. This might mean running social media campaigns to raise awareness about ministry work or a free internet café to address the digital divide in a positive way. Identifying core values also reveals patterns of spiritual life advocated by the community that might conflict with certain technologies. Highly liturgical worship communities that value embodied worship, for example, will always find mediated, online worship lacking or problematic. They may consider some sacramental acts like Communion theologically inauthentic when performed in a digital environment. Therefore, highlighting core communal values helps draw attention to both the potential and the challenges of new media use for a given group, suggesting what forms of engagement a given tradition might innately encourage or discourage.

In a culture dominated by digital technologies, people of faith need to understand not only the interworking of new media but also how their religious values can create certain trajectories of media usage. This starts by reflecting on a group's religious identity, including naming its mission statement and values. Once these have been identified, it is important to ask, How might these values reflect a certain belief about or position toward media? Unpacking one's core values helps clarify not only religious priorities but also how these beliefs call one to engage or resist certain aspects of new media technology and culture. Religious communities often encounter internal tensions or heated debates regarding technology use because community members propose that new media be used in ways that run counter to the values of the group, or because the members seeking to employ technology do not fully understand the historic identity or ethos of the community. Thus, having an informed understanding of a community's identity can help highlight potential positive technological uses or points of conflict for a given group.

Media Negotiation: Accepting, Rejecting, and Innovating Technology in Light of Faith

Layers one and two help uncover the essential background information of the identity and ethos of a given group and spotlight its values platform. This helps us contextualize the group's media evaluation and choices. Mapping out the historical and theological tradition of a community provides us with key clues as to what its response to technologies may or should be. From this basis we can begin to look at the media negotiation process itself. The religious social-shaping approach to technology recognizes that religious communities do not reject technology outright. Rather, they may reject certain uses of a given technology, certain messages sent through that technology, or certain values that technology is seen to encourage.

In considering the negotiation process, we must start with the assumption that a specific Christian community will neither fully accept nor fully reject any technology, thus calling for careful analysis of the specific aspects and uses of each technology and their outcomes. We must focus on what specific aspects of the technology are deemed useful and acceptable in light of the communal mission, what aspects are problematic and worth rejecting because of the values they encourage or undermine, and the extent to which the technology may call for some kind of reconfiguring in light of the community's value platform. Paying attention to this process of negotiation means identifying both the positive and negative affordances a given technology offers a community in light of its particular values. It also requires considering how a community's response takes into account how these affordances interact with the moral and ethical boundaries of the community and the technology itself.

One way to study media negotiation is to look at examples of how members of a specific tradition use new media. By observing their motivation for media use or innovation, we can more easily highlight what aspects of technology use are seen as beneficial or acceptable to a given group. For example, during the past two years, #ashtag and #showyourash hashtags have emerged as a way to encourage clergy and parishioners to post selfies of themselves observing Ash Wednesday via social media.[13] Selfies of people from all walks of life with ceremonial ash crosses on their foreheads are shared on platforms such as Facebook, Twitter, and Instagram. This trend shows that many Catholics, Episcopalians, Lutherans, and others see social media as an acceptable and popular way to communicate their religious identities and make public declarations of faith. Such practices both model and highlight acceptable uses of the internet for religious purposes, especially when they encourage Christians to demonstrate and make visible their faith within broader society through digital media use.

Studying media negotiation can also involve looking at initiatives sponsored by specific Christian groups. For example, the BigBible Project (http://bigbible.org.uk/), which is supported by the Methodist church in the United Kingdom, seeks to get people interested in Bible reading by using digital resources that allow them to share their thoughts online and by providing resources for approaching the digital age from a biblical perspective. This is done through a blog focused on getting readers to engage more deeply with the Bible, an annual #MediaLit course providing practical training on the workings of media, and helping organize the Christian New Media Awards and Conference, which offers sessions on theological reflection on digital media's impact on society and spotlights Christians doing innovative ministry online.

As we have seen, those wishing to reflect on this negotiation process should start by considering in what ways the forms of media under reflection mirror past technologies or debates to see if any previous decisions, guidelines, or community discourse may be applied to this decision making. If the qualities, outcomes, or social conditions created by a new technology are significantly unique, the individual or community must enter into a rigorous process to determine what aspects of the technology can be accepted and which ones might need to be rejected or reconstructed. When considering the decision-making process regarding new media technologies, people of faith must address several key questions:

- What values do those media applications seem to promote?
- Do they complement or contradict Christian values or identity?
- Which features or forms of new media are most useful in the mission of your group?
- Are there features of new media, or values associated with them, that are problematic for your group?

Responses to such questions begin to reveal communal priorities and help clarify how to move forward in relation to the possibilities and challenges the technology offers for a given group. Such questioning also reveals whether or not innovation is required. If a technology is viewed as valuable but is seen to possess some problematic qualities, then the technology must be altered to align with community beliefs and practices. Such reflection not only provides a basis for a theologically informed response but also makes room for religious innovation and creativity within new media technologies.

Community Discourse about Technology: Talking about Technology as an Expression of Religious Identity

Finally, we must look at the communal framing and discourse resulting from the adoption or adaptation of a given technology. This fourth layer of reflection involves examining how religious communities talk about their technological choices. While this has often been overlooked in studies of the social shaping of technology, it is crucial. The act of creating internal or external discourses plays an essential role within religious communities, providing justification for their approach to new media. Within the religious-social shaping approach to technology, scholars are encouraged to consider how uses and implications of new technologies may require a community and its leaders to amend their previous views or official policies related to media. The negotiation and adoption of new technologies often require religious groups to create distinctive public and private discourses to validate their technology choices, as well as discourses to support and promote already established community boundaries, values, and identities.

Thus, a community's discourse about technology plays a dual role. Technology talk within the group becomes a tool to affirm community identity and boundaries. Technology talk can also be used as a public relations exercise to show how a religious group positions itself in relation to contemporary culture and values, promoting a certain perception of the group to the wider world. It also helps establish a current and future media trajectory for the group, clarifying how media decisions connect to established communal values and providing informed guidance for the future.

Paying attention to the language and debates used by a religious community to frame technology and prescribe communal use is a crucial part of this discernment and process of analysis. This can involve a close reading of the official documents, media resource material, or sermons of a given community to help unpack its motivations and beliefs regarding the internet and evaluate how such instruction offers insights into the religious identity it seeks to present. Christian denominations that have created official statements or position papers regarding how the internet should be used and perceived by their membership offer useful places to begin such investigation. For example, over the years the United Methodist Church has produced a number of statements and reports in its annual *Book of Resolutions* related to how computers and the internet affect the social community of the church and the world. In its 2004 statement titled "Proper Use of Information Communication Technologies," the church draws on the Methodist social justice tradition to highlight the rights and the responsibility of humanity to act in fairness toward one another within the larger human community in the use of digital technologies and the treatment of others online. The Roman Catholic Church also offers official media guidelines for church practice related to the media. The Pontifical Council for Social Communications, mentioned in an earlier chapter, is responsible for publishing papal encyclicals on media, such as *The Church and Internet* and *Ethics in Internet*, which spell out a distinct theology of communication related to the internet for this religious community.[14] Such documents often combine practical advice with theological justifications, meaning they offer an important resource to help identify a community's values related to media in contemporary society. Yet many groups do not have such clear statements from which to analyze and draw such conclusions. This means looking at other sources, such as sermons that offer insight into a community's beliefs about media or the discourse around media initiatives that a community is involved in or supports. One alternative is to look at broader initiatives with which specific groups may link themselves, such as Internet Evangelism Day, an event that takes place in April each year with the intent to encourage churches and Christian organizations to take time one Sunday each year to offer trainings and facilitate discussions about online evangelism. The initiative's online resources (found at www.internetevangelismday.com) spell out distinct beliefs about how the internet should be used as a tool for missions. Such sources can prove helpful to identify the technology talk of a specific group and how a group performs or acts out their identity in public spaces.

When moving toward religiously informed decision making regarding technology, one must take advantage of the opportunity to consciously articulate such decisions in light of one's faith community and perspective. Here it is essential to ask: In what ways can social media complement your mission and present a certain view of Christians in contemporary society? Technology use informed by an individual's or group's religious identity can become a powerful occasion for representing religion in the public sphere as words meet with faithfully informed action. Also, increasingly in digital culture, some religious groups are issuing policy statements or guidelines about technology as a way to offer their members advice on how to use new media in ways that support the values of their group. This may be a statement of proper netiquette (internet etiquette) on a group's website or guides to online communication (such as the United Methodist Church's "Group Email Netiquette" statement); statements about using social media for missions (such as resources and examples provided by the Internet Evangelism Day website, including "Facebook and Evangelism," www.internetevangelismday.com/facebook-evangelism.php); or even documents that outline ethical Christian responses to new media culture (such as the Vatican's *Church and Internet* statement cited above). These discourse statements typically speak as much to the values of the particular group they represent and how it seeks to live out its faith as they do about a particular technology and its use. Paying attention to how someone talks about technology can and should reveal who one seeks to be as a Christian and what a Christian response to technology and to the wider digital culture should or could look like.

For a particular group to move toward a personal statement or official position, it is important to consider whether any media and technology policies or guidelines already exist and whether these need to be revised or more widely articulated. If nothing like these exists, one might consider whether they need to be drafted in a way that clearly articulates spiritual values/mission and technological belief and how these complement one another. Communal discourse about technology gives a group the opportunity not only to reflect on a certain position or create a statement about a new technology but also to use technology talk as a way to reaffirm Christian identity and beliefs.

Summary: Toward a Communal Theological Reflection on New Media

Together, these four levels of inquiry provide a framework for religious individuals and organizations to think through what a Christian response to new media might look like for them. But what might this process actually look like in practice? The starting point is the assumption that if we are going to make theologically informed decisions about technology—especially in a world where digital, networked technologies are embedded in our everyday lives—we must start by understanding our Christian and communal history and identity. In many sectors of the church, biblical literacy and understanding of the Christian tradition are quite low. As it says on the front of the National Archives in Washington, DC, "What is past is prologue." If we are to understand our negotiation with technological culture, we must start by understanding what the Christian faith has to say about engagement with culture in general. We must be aware of the roots of our faith to know how our tradition emerged within the world and to understand the theological resources our faith offers us for life in today's society. Second, we must be aware of the current culture and society we are a part of. One purpose of this book has been to unpack and reveal the values of digital culture, in which our faith has become situated. We must devote the same careful attention to uncovering and reflecting on the theological beliefs and values that should guide our technological decision-making processes and the life of faith in a network society.

With this base information clearly in mind, we can move to the third point of reflection, considering how these values and background set out particular negotiation strategies, routes, and trajectories in relation to specific technologies. As stated above, many religious communities often face tension regarding whether or not to adopt or engage with a new form of media, because the choices recommended, the design of a platform, or the options offered run counter to the tradition, values, or priorities of the particular Christian group. The intent to use new media in a certain way may be innovative and potentially in line with a group's Christian ethos, but a tension arises as the use or innovation may highlight competing agendas at work or divergent values within different sectors of the group. If the proposed use is based on a misunderstanding of the technology being negotiated or of the perceived ethos of the particular group, then it may not be in tune with the group's mission or even the Christian tradition.

Finally, when we find that media negotiation offers us opportunities for technology adoption and innovation that augment faith, we can move toward potentially creating an official statement or position articulating how media usage complements and enhances the life of faith. Technology talk offers the chance for an individual or group to say, "This is our website (or social-media strategy or religious app), these are our core beliefs, and this is how we see technology and digital culture in light of what we are called to seek and who we are called to be." This creates a great opportunity for churches and religious communities, because it is not simply a chance to proclaim who we are in Christ to the world but also an opportunity to reflect on who we are called to be in contemporary culture. Technology talk becomes an opportunity for both internal reflection and external proclamation. This suggests that Christian groups need to be actively engaged in developing ways to use new technologies for Christian mission and practice and also in developing theologically informed statements about technology.

In summary, to move toward a theologically informed response to technology, we must consider two central questions. First, what factors and beliefs are held by your church or community that might influence your community's response to technology? This means identifying the teachings within Christianity that can serve as resources to help inform the ways we should think about technology and talk to other people about living faithfully with technology. Second, what tensions might new media pose to Christian community? Considering the tensions new media can cause may reveal the places where new media and digital literacy are needed or where technological choices need to be altered to support the callings and mandates of Christian community.

engaging appropriately with technology and media

Appropriate Technology as Public Theology

Our reflection on Christian faith and its intersection with technology and media leads to questions about appropriate engagement with technology, and this brings us into the space of public theology. Discussions of an appropriate response to technology have a clear ethical dimension as they overlap with questions such as "How should I live?" and "How ought we to live?" The quest for the "good life," theologian Stanley Grenz contends, is rooted in a living consciousness of who God is, who we are, what it means to be followers of Christ, and what God's trajectory for the world at large is.[1] Because technology and media can be thought of as tools or instruments as well as the environments we live in, engagement with them connects to both private and public worlds. As we discussed in chapter 3 in relation to our digital culture, this is an engagement with a multisite reality demanding both individual and social ethics. Technological decision making takes place not only in our individual lives but also in our neighborhoods and all of network society wherever human life interacts.

We argue that technological decision making is a form of public theology. Our reflection on what we consider appropriate technology and media is linked to an understanding of the role and context of public theology. Political theologian Duncan Forrester describes public theology as follows:

> Theology seeks the welfare of the city before protecting the interests of the Church, or its proper liberty to preach the Gospel and celebrate the sacraments. Accordingly, public theology often takes "the world's agenda," or parts of it, as its own agenda, and seeks to offer distinctive and constructive insights from the treasury of faith to help in the building of a decent society, the restraint of evil, the curbing of violence, nation-building, and reconciliation in the public arena, and so forth. It strives to offer something that is distinctive, and that is gospel, rather than simply adding the voice of theology to what everyone is saying already. Thus it seeks to deploy theology in public debate, rather than a vague and optimistic idealism which tends to disintegrate in the face of radical evil.[2]

Broadly speaking, this means the world sets the agenda for a public theology. In our case it helps focus our attention on how technology and media are being engaged and viewed in wider society. This focus is then framed by issues and concerns that theological insight and worldviews bring to our attention. This process is discussed by theologian Paul Tillich in his "method of correction," by which he suggests our everyday lives raise questions, particularly about who we are, and theology draws upon its unique set of resources to answer those questions in a language understood by the everyday world.[3] For example, technology and media used in the everyday world might raise questions about what authentic human relationships look like, how we are treated and treat others in technologically mediated contexts, and the value of the human person. The heart of public theology is a community of faith, informed by Scripture and tradition, committed to reading the "signs of the times," and acting for the common good of all individuals and the wider society.[4] Thinking theologically about technology and media in the context of public theology involves thinking about how our understanding of technology and media might offer a distinctive and constructive approach that can enrich wider society, especially in ways that help restrain evil and violence and promote building communities of reconciliation.

This theological approach is based on two key assertions: no sacred/secular divide limits the bounds of theological engagement, and the fundamental source of our response is the gospel of Jesus Christ.[5] The first assertion understands that if Jesus Christ is Lord of the heavens and the earth and all that is in them, then there is no division between "sacred" and "secular." Theological voices are thus faithfully required to speak in all contexts of the world and act accordingly. Kathryn Tanner echoes this when she asserts that theology must be comprehensive in its exploration of what it means to be human beings in relationship with God, for if God is the Lord of everything, then no aspect of the world, no matter how ordinary, is exempt from being understood in relation to faith.[6] The second assertion, derived from the first, states that Christian beliefs about God, human nature, and destiny, along with the values that arise from these, should shape public policy and life.

Together these assertions form the basis of a public theology, which exists within a contested space. The negotiations between theology, technology, and media occur not just in church communities but within the broader public square outside those communities. This public space is contested because, while Western liberal democracies argue strongly for free access to public space under the principle of democratic participation, access to that space does not guarantee a positive reception of one's speech. Therefore, Christian perspectives on appropriate technology and media need to be told in ways that are both credible and intelligible to a wider public that no longer holds to Christian theology and its sources as authoritative, unique, or a public truth.[7]

As we engage with technology and media in both the private and public spaces of life, we also will engage with more than one kind of public space. Theologian David Tracy divides "public" into three distinct spaces: church, academy, and society.[8] But our discussions are not limited to these three publics. Other social configurations exist, such as a threefold public of the state (local government, national government, state welfare), civil society (charities, faith communities, voluntary bodies), and the market (including business, finance, corporations). Another definition sees the "public" simply as anything outside the church or other religious institutions. Each public space has its own particular forms of language and engagement, and these must be identified by those communicating what they think is the good news of Jesus Christ for a given space into their respective discussions.[9] Conversations about how we ought to live will have different flavors within these different contexts, though there will be some common features to them.

Thus, when thinking about an appropriate response to technology in light of a public theology, we must start by discerning the specific context we are examining. What is it, we must ask, that the Christian tradition can offer here in light of the good news of Jesus Christ? And how can it offer it in a way that is intelligible and credible to those in that context and also valuable and relevant to their everyday lives? All of these factors are critical for our theologizing about technology and media if it is to have a very real presence.[10]

Therefore, wrestling with what is or is not appropriate technology and media has two key components. The first is a deep theological reflection about both the technology in question and the context in which it is situated. The second is the task of deciding how to faithfully communicate the product of that reflection in a way that is credible and intelligible to the particular public being engaged.

We suggest that a networked theology involves a twofold movement: we receive revelation from God that provides us with a baseline for engaging with the everyday, including the technological world, and then these principles are realized and articulated through our personal convictions that are situated within our broader community of faith.[11] This is similar to Douglas Hall's contention that a significant part of the theological process is finding out about the Christian theological past, but this exploration becomes authentic theology only "when what has been received is appropriated, made our own. For that to happen, the received tradition must of course pass through the sieve of our own individual and contemporary-collective experience; we cannot give it, profess it as ours, unless such a process occurs."[12] This means, for example, that we receive the narratives and examples of neighborliness found in Scripture, such as in the parable of the good Samaritan. However, these scriptural norms or principles of neighborliness and love remain impotent until worked out through the personal convictions of people in the contexts where they work, live, play, and worship.

This understanding can be extended to the way in which religious communities negotiate the presence and use of new media technologies in light of decisions made in past negotiations with media.[13] This echoes the religious-social shaping of technology approach outlined in the previous chapter. This approach argues that in mapping out a communal theological response to technology, we must consider both the historical context and the contemporary moment of a given community to inform its choices related to technology.

Paying attention to the contexts in which our reflection on media and technology occurs prompts us to ask how we should speak in these public contexts. For example, we could take a "common currency" approach, where we recognize that "God talk" and faith-based language may put up barriers to communication, and so we look for some sort of common ground in terms of issues or values to establish a dialogue between others and ourselves. In other words, we identify how media and technology use intersect with broader ideas of what human well-being and flourishing look like while we are "wrapped in media." This approach can be problematic, though, in that it suggests that faith perspectives are not actually necessary for a common good to be achieved, and so Christian distinctiveness can be lost. An alternative approach is to attempt to "out narrate" competing stories in the public square about how to live with technology and media by offering a "distinctive discourse" rooted in the language of faith.[14] In this case, the strategy is for Christian communities to create and live lifestyles around technology and media so demonstrably life-giving, engaging, and respectful of the other that it becomes a better or more convincing story than those being told or modeled by others outside the church.

Another option is to try to combine the two approaches above with a view to establishing common ground or dialogue as well as maintaining a distinctly Christian voice.[15] This approach looks first to establish a dialogue with various other parties around common issues presented by technology. In establishing this, though, we do not hide our faith perspective or mention God so late as to lose the Christian identity of our contribution. The challenge is to create a vision of appropriate technology that finds common ground in its starting point but is unashamedly Christian and Christ-following in its ethos and how it is lived out in the world. We engage with the wider world by speaking a language that can be understood by others, but with a distinct accent of faith. Our goal in dialoguing with others around media and technology is to offer something uniquely Christian.

Faithful, Appropriate Technology

The challenge, we have seen, is to create a Christ-infused vision of what an appropriate response to technology could look like, one that can be communicated intelligibly and credibly to both church communities as well as wider publics. We suggest beginning by returning to the questions around neighbors and neighborhoods considered earlier. This involves identifying what values should be at the heart of those considerations, and how particular people and communities have used values to shape their technological and media engagement.

A significant theological attempt to identify a core set of values for this kind of approach to technology was proposed by science and religion scholar Ian Barbour. Barbour described technology that is appropriate for humanity as a "creative technology that is economically productive, ecologically sound, socially just, and personally fulfilling."[16] At the heart of this definition is Barbour's contention that personal needs, including individual autonomy, personal relationships, and even spirituality, must be maintained in the face of technological development. Those personal needs, however, are situated within a set of values oriented toward wider social and environmental contexts. Given that, the voices of all those affected by technological power need to be heard by those who wield it. Part of this, Barbour maintains, requires examining how technology has been used in the past, in a way that shapes its future trajectory in both human and environmental contexts, including the costs in both human and environmental terms. It also requires looking beyond narrow economic and pragmatic agendas.

Ideally, Barbour suggests, technology that is appropriate harnesses some of the benefits proposed by those who are optimistic about technology and see it as a liberator, while also avoiding the negative human and environmental costs asserted by the pessimists who see technology as an oppressor. Such a balanced approach to technology identifies and incorporates local values, knowledge, and materials to build appropriately scaled systems for the local community. These systems in turn connect to a wider technological environment in a manner similar to Nardi and O'Day's ecological representation of technology mentioned earlier. This environment is a dynamic system comprised of people, practices, values, and technologies, which make up overlapping subsystems and feedback loops. It grows, shrinks, adapts, and evolves over time because of both its internal life and the way it interfaces with technological systems on a global level.[17] Appropriate technology recognizes that technology can be a powerful force for good as well as oppression, and it promotes political and social discussion over technology's impact. For example, in the case of surveillance noted previously, digital communications technologies can aid in locating missing persons, solving crimes, and protecting freedom, human lives, and livelihoods, but they can simultaneously be used to remove individual and community privacy, coerce individuals and communities, and take away freedom. Appropriate technology also recognizes the values local communities have in negotiating technological development and implementation. Thus, it carries the idea of technology bringing economic development and material production, coupled with social and environmental concern.

Expanding the Spiritual Dimensions of Appropriate Technology

Barbour's definition of appropriate technology is a helpful starting point for thinking about how we might faithfully engage with media and technology in ways that are creative, economically productive, ecologically sound, socially just, and personally fulfilling. We must now unpack this in terms of particular values and worldviews that lead to an engagement with technology and media that stands in continuity with the Christian faith and, in particular, is Christ-centered. We begin by reflecting on human creativity, economic production, ecological matters, social justice, and personal fulfillment in terms of media and technology. What are some of the biblical and theological foundations for doing this? How might those foundations be worked out through concrete examples?

Christian spirituality must include an awareness of technology and media and their effects upon our faith communities and our world. That awareness enables us to engage critically with them and to integrate them into our lives in a way that aligns with an understanding of the call to follow Christ and to seek God's kingdom here on earth. This is a form of spirituality, a lived experience of the Christian faith in a technological world, that moves beyond a syncretistic assimilation of Christian faith by technology and media, where the priorities and values of technology and media become portrayed as an uncritical expression of Christianity, and technology has become "baptized" by Christianity. Instead, it moves toward a genuine dialogue between technology and Christian beliefs, values, and practices in order to bring about sustainable, wise, and life-giving ways of life for individuals and communities both inside and outside the church.

In previous chapters we have referred to several biblical starting points for thinking about technology and media, including the idea of human beings as created in the image of God and Jesus's commandments to love God and love our neighbors. To these we will add another biblical starting point that highlights particular aspects of what loving God, loving neighbor, and recognizing the humanity of others looks like. At the start of Jesus's ministry, as recorded in the Gospel of Luke, Jesus describes what the good news he has come to proclaim looks like. In Luke 4 Jesus takes the scroll of the prophet Isaiah and reads aloud:

> The Spirit of the Lord is upon me,
> because he has anointed me
> to bring good news to the poor.
> He has sent me to proclaim release to the captives
> and recovery of sight to the blind,
> to let the oppressed go free,
> to proclaim the year of the Lord's favor.
> (vv. 18–19)

Jesus's ministry is tied to his self-identification as the agent through whom captives and the oppressed are freed, good news is proclaimed to the poor, and the blind are healed. Biblical scholar Darrell Bock comments that the message of freedom that this text proclaims is so radical and powerful, challenging as it does the established status quo in any and all societies, that it has become the central text shaping not only social concern but also engagement with oppressive political and social systems.[18] For all who follow Christ and are called to reflect him in the everyday world, the passage raises the question of what this should look like in a world of networked media and technology environments. In particular, it raises key questions about who the "poor" are in an information society, how they might be suffering and oppressed technologically, and what our response in Christ is to address that. We move beyond trite questions like "Would Jesus use social media?" to a more profound reflection on how to mirror the character of Christ in how we live with and talk about technology and media.

To integrate these various biblical and theological principles into an appropriate Christ-informed response to technology and media, we can return to the text from Micah 6:8 (NIV): "He has shown you, O mortal, what is good. And what does the LORD require of you? To act justly and to love mercy and to walk humbly with your God." Here we are presented with a call to do three concrete things: to do justice, to love kindness and mercy, and to walk humbly with God. Biblical scholar Walter Brueggemann asserts that these are three important dimensions of the life of faith, which mutually support one another.[19] Each of these aspects is about relationships: our relationship with God, our relationship with other people, and our relationship with God's creation. This can be expanded to include our relationship with technology and media. These three dimensions of life encompass the other themes we have discussed: of being image bearers of Christ, loving God and neighbor, and proclaiming the good news of Jesus in a technological and media world.

Doing Justice

The call to justice is broader than a concern with punishing those who do wrong or oppress people. It is about living your life in right relationships with others. It is an active task, something to be worked at constantly. It involves moving beyond condemning those who take advantage of or marginalize others and instead being part of the process that raises up those people and restores them to full life in community. The terms "righteousness" (in Hebrew, *tsedaqah*) and "justice" (in Hebrew, *mishpat*) permeate much of the Hebrew Scriptures, especially the prophetic writings. Succinctly put, righteousness entails the idea of something that truly fulfills its purpose, something that is true to its calling and matches a norm, and justice is linked to what needs to be done in a particular situation for this fullness of purpose to be restored. Human beings are called to be God's image bearers in the world, and living righteously would see that image bearing carried out in such a way as fulfills God's purpose for that situation. In this context, justice serves to establish the environment where the fullness of image bearing can be lived out in accordance with that purpose.

These two terms are closely related to the concepts of holiness (in Hebrew, *qodesh*) and faithfulness (in Hebrew, *hesed*). Holiness highlights God's absoluteness and perfection in being righteous and just (e.g., Isa. 5:16), and faithfulness speaks of an unshakable covenant loyalty to others (e.g., Ps. 36:10). Together, these four terms interact to bring about the state of wholeness (in Hebrew, *shalom*) in every dimension of life. It is this wholeness that God desires for God's people and God's world.[20] As Duncan Forrester points out, justice is expressed in social relationships as the very substance of faith, not just its application. Justice, therefore, moves beyond just the application of some principles of the Christian faith to become the how and why of living.[21] As such, prophetic voices in the Christian tradition seek to draw the people of God, past and present, back to a way of life that is shaped by righteousness and justice and offers hope and freedom within that life for individuals and communities.

Loving Mercy

The how and why of living is born out of a commitment to loving mercy or kindness. This means being faithfully and actively committed to others in the same way that God is faithful in his loving kindness (*hesed*) toward the world and all in it. It goes beyond acts of charity and compassion to those in need and describes the relationship we are to have with God and each other. This ideal relationship should display grace, generosity, and loyalty to those around us and in the wider community. This part of life, *hesed*, with its strong relational aspect of loyalty, faithfulness, and steadfast love toward one another, might even be seen as the essence of God's covenants with his people, where God remains faithful to his people in spite of their failure to maintain their side of the relationship and their walking away from him.[22]

Walking Humbly

Both justice and mercy are worked out in the prophet's call to walk humbly with God, recognizing our dependence on God for all things and trusting God first before our own human ingenuity. Gary Smith describes this walk as a "warning against carelessly or presumptuously doing things your own way, instead of being attentive to do God's will."[23] This statement echoes the theme running through the biblical book of Proverbs, where acknowledging the reality of who God is and your own status in relation to God is the beginning of human wisdom and understanding for right relationships and personal and communal well-being (Prov. 9:10).

Coming back to our question about what an appropriate relationship with technology and media might look like, we suggest that Micah's charge offers a useful starting point. Our response to technology should not only be economically productive, ecologically sound, socially just, and personally fulfilling. It should also include a call to act justly, be authentic and wholesome in our relationships, and walk in line with God in our technological world. This prophetic call also enables us to identify where the strengths of technology might be used to undo its oppressive nature and aid the poor and oppressed in this world.

Appropriate engagement with technology and media contributes not just to an appropriate personal use of these but also to the development of wider human well-being and flourishing. This is in part captured by the notion of *shalom* mentioned above. *Shalom* is commonly concerned with a state of physical or material well-being, where things are as they should be, and is linked to a sense of prosperity as well as to safety and security of physical, material life. The presence of *shalom* adds a moral or ethical dimension tied to honesty and authenticity in human relationships.[24] In the following section, we look at some examples of how these ideas of justice, kindness, and walking humbly with God might be located in our networked theology, and how an orientation to *shalom*, found in the good news of Jesus Christ, might be worked out in our technological practice. This call to promote justice, mercy, and humility through our technological engagement sets out a unique platform from which we can more carefully explore how individual Christians can evaluate and create a networked theological response to technology.

Engaging Technology and Media Appropriately

This book has sought to define and examine new media and digital technologies in relation to the Christian faith. Through this exploration we have noted various approaches or attitudes toward media, positive and negative, and have seen technologies as value-neutral or value-laden instruments and environments. We have also asserted that the development of new media elicits processes of negotiation in religious communities around the adoption of these media, especially in light of prior negotiations of older media, and that the concept of neighborliness provides a set of questions to engage that negotiation. The aim is to provide a clear basis for evaluating the adoption and use of technology and media that is consistent with the Christian hope of the coming fullness of the kingdom of God, with all that entails in terms of love of God and love of neighbor.

It can be argued that humans, including their engagement with technology and media, are called to anticipate the perfection found in the fullness of the kingdom present on the other side of the eschatological horizon marked by Jesus's return. This is the opinion of science and religion scholar Robert Russell. Russell argues that the new creation and way of life seen in the resurrection of Jesus Christ, and the future hope generated by this event, should shape the values and goals of all Christian technological endeavors. There is an ethical dimension to human technological decision making that is inspired by the promise of God for a future where the world is free from death, pain, and sadness (Rev. 21:4), and a world of *shalom* is brought into being. "It is this eschatological future—no matter how dim, how inconceivable it is in light of science, no matter how unlikely it is in light of evil and suffering in human society and nature—to which we must orient all our ultimate plans and ideals and convictions if we are to live as Christians today in the Easter dawning of a new age."[25]

Thus, our approach to an appropriate understanding of technology is shaped by this anticipation of the kingdom found in our Christian hope, as well as the hope found in a present that can be transformed by the love of Christ. The world of redemption is ultimately focused on God's action, seen in the work of Christ and the Holy Spirit, as an act of grace that inspires human activity in the world. We are called to act as the God who redeems acts, or as Russell puts it, to become "eschatological companions" with God in the world. In the discussions that follow, we bring the different strands of doing justice, loving mercy, and walking humbly with God together with the aspects of neighborliness discussed in chapter 4. By looking at how these intersect with our discussion of appropriate technology as seen through biblical and theological lenses, we offer some specific spaces where people of faith can actively and concretely evaluate their personal responses to and engagement with digital media and environments.

Serving Justice through Right Relationships

At its heart, doing justice is about living our lives in right relationship with others by working to challenge and resist the marginalization of others and restore others into the fullness of life. What matters is doing justice—committed action in the world shaped by God's concern for justice and compassion—not just believing in an intellectual version of it. This sense of justice as transformative action is present throughout Christianity and hinges on the understanding that individuals, communities, and the wider world matter to God. Traditions such as Roman Catholicism and Protestantism might place different emphases on the roles of church leaders, tradition, reason, and scriptural understandings of justice, but both groups as followers of Christ are called explicitly to do justice.

Roman Catholic teachings on justice, and particularly social justice, are drawn from various sources, including papal works, decisions, and documents of Vatican councils and various bishops' conferences, particularly from the past one hundred years. Papal materials tend to focus on issues concerning the wider world and the universal church, while more particular or local concerns and issues are often the focus of bishops' conferences. For example, Paul VI's encyclical *Humanae Vitae* (1968) dealt with the broad scope of human reproduction, and the Latin American bishops' conference in Medellín in 1968 focused on issues of poverty and liberation in the Latin American context. Each of these sources uses the others, as well as biblical material, to produce a diverse and loosely integrated body of work.

While the range of social teaching is diverse, the core principles of social transformation and human dignity are held in common. First, inherent in the believer's relationship with God is the command that faith be engaged with every aspect of the everyday world, whether that be socially, politically, culturally, or economically. The good news of Jesus Christ is not merely proclaimed in words but is lived out in the life of every person in the church. This view is seen in the often-cited opening sentence of an international synod of Roman Catholic bishops in 1971: "Action on behalf of justice and participation in the transformation of the world fully appear to us as a constitutive dimension of the preaching of the Gospel, or, in other words, of the church's mission for the redemption of the human race and its liberation from every oppressive situation."[26]

A second principle in Catholic social teaching is that human dignity, which is realized in social relationships or community, is of utmost value. Again, this principle is rooted in the doctrine that human beings are made in the image of God, which points to an inherent dignity, and even sacramental value, in each person. This dignity, sourced in the divine created order, is then linked to a call to become part of a community of wholeness and justice that God covenants through Jesus Christ with all the people of the world. As such, this vision of humanity sees each person, both as an individual and as part of a community, as possessing inherent human rights and responsibilities toward others. It also recognizes that sin affects not only individual lives but also all human relationships and therefore the structures and institutions of society. Thus, the Christian is called to respond to individual human suffering through charity while also seeking to transform society's structures into something more wholesome and just.[27]

Catholic understandings of human dignity draw predominantly from a natural law approach, which argues that human self-interest is transcended by the divine natural order, an order that can be recognized by human reason. This view that one can look at the world around us and, through the use of human reason, discern a moral framework for living sits uncomfortably with Protestant Christianity.[28] Protestant Christianity tends to be suspicious of human reason, seeing it as influenced by sin, and so often looks first to the biblical texts for its understanding of justice. This is not to say that philosophical thought is ignored within the Protestant tradition. Martin Luther, for example, uses philosophy in regard to sociopolitical engagement, but theologically it is downplayed.

A theme drawn from the biblical texts that runs through Protestant thinking about human agency is that the gospel is to be transformative of both church and society. The transformation of society through individual and communal action is a response to the grace received from God's saving action. Grace is unmerited, in that it cannot be earned by human effort, but upon receiving it from God through faith, the Christian is called to respond to that grace in the pattern of a responsible, obedient life oriented toward God. Charity, acts of justice, and working for the common good of society are linked to seeking God's will. They become "works of righteousness" through which that will is lived out as they align with both the biblical examples and Christ's teaching and life.[29]

While Catholicism and Protestantism have different influences on their understandings of justice and social concern, many of the biblical texts mentioned previously are core to both traditions' understandings of personal and social justice. These include the prophets such as Isaiah, Micah, and Amos, as well as the wider tradition involving the law (e.g., Exod. 22:22–24, 26), the Psalms (e.g., Ps. 146:7–9), and Wisdom literature (e.g., Prov. 14:31; 22:22–23). These passages call for people to be involved in restoring wholeness to individuals and communities who are poor and oppressed, to speak out and act against injustice, and to do this in response to our Creator and Sustainer who is the source of true righteousness, justice, and wholeness.[30]

As noted above, the doctrine that humans bear the image and likeness of God, drawn from Genesis 1:26–28, is a key biblical theme developed in respect to justice. For some, the Genesis text has served as a starting point to assert a community of equals across humanity by drawing upon the universality of the *imago Dei* in both female and male. Various liberation theologians see this particular biblical text, together with the exodus narrative, as critical to Christian faith and practice. The theme of the goodness of creation and God's concern for it also runs through both Hebrew and Christian writings, leading to the Christian understanding of creation being redeemed through Jesus Christ. This interpretation ascribes a value to the environment and all within it that influences social concern and can critique excessive anthropocentricism, or human-centeredness. All of these themes are picked up in both Protestant and Catholic traditions to provide a prophetic voice that evaluates society on the basis of how it treats the weak and the poor, with an emphasis on responding actively to issues of injustice faced by individuals and communities.[31]

Jesus's claim to bring abundant life (John 10:10), combined with the passage from Luke 4 about Jesus's mission to free the captives, release the oppressed, and heal the blind, points forward to the full realization of God's justice in the future, which will bring about true wholeness of individuals and communities. Justice is always set into an eschatological framework, from Amos's bleak "day of the Lord" (Amos 5), where those who oppress will be judged by God, to Jesus's anticipation of the fullness of the kingdom of God, and finally to the apocalyptic vision of the Revelation of John. In Revelation, descriptions of judgment are followed by the consequent abolition of suffering, sickness, and death for the people of God and creation (e.g., Rev. 20–21). For Forrester, doing justice here in the present is to anticipate the coming kingdom of God, to aspire to its vision of wholeness, and to have hope in God's ultimate justice.

> This hope is at its heart and throughout social. The principal images used for the future are not those of the flight of the alone to the Alone, of the soul's ascent to God, but the powerful symbols of the Reign of God for the coming of which we pray, the City that believers seek whose builder and maker is God, the New Jerusalem, that comes down out of heaven from God. These images all suggest a coming just ordering of relationships; in hope we look forward to the future triumph of righteousness and justice. The hope also has judgment at its heart; there is here no evasion of the gravity of sin and offence, oppression and injustice. In the City, in the New Jerusalem, justice will be enthroned. In judgment the poor and the weak are to be vindicated and upheld. This hope challenges the existing orders of injustice, violence, and brutality. The hope is good news to the poor and all who suffer.[32]

In the Christian tradition, God's justice is seen as being made manifest in the person and work of Jesus Christ. Here is the one who through the incarnation, his life, teaching, suffering, death, and resurrection worked to restore the world to a relationship of wholeness with God that will be consummated at the eschaton. Jesus Christ's concern is for wholeness for all, and especially for those who are oppressed and marginalized. He is both the example and the destination for social concern and justice. Ultimately, justice, together with final redemption, is God's prerogative, and human beings are called to act in similarly just and redemptive ways in all of life, including in our appropriation and use of technology.

Serving Justice through Technology

What does a networked theology need to pay attention to in relation to the call to do justice in a technological world? The key to answering that question is to ask who is, or might be, marginalized in our use of technology and media. Which individuals or communities have their humanity diminished and become objects rather than subjects? We might think of this in broad terms of how our use of technology and media may disenfranchise entire communities, diminishing their participation in wider society, whether that be economically, academically, or socially. Equally, we might examine the effects, or the potential effects, of our practices on particular individuals.

For example, moving government or commercial services to an online mode accessible through phone or web applications may improve the overall management of the bureaucratic system, but it may also exclude the very people it intends to serve. Those without the financial, educational, or technological means to access and use that system effectively to seek aid and assistance (e.g., social welfare, banking) or to perform tasks required of them as citizens (e.g., paying taxes, voting) can cease to function well as citizens. Moreover, such systems themselves have the potential (and often reality) of reducing flesh-and-blood human beings to simply "clients," "cases," or ID numbers, removing their personhood in the process.

One area where issues of technological justice become tangible relates to the discussion of access to technology. This is often framed around the idea of the "digital divide," which describes how, in an information age and economy, our world is increasingly being split into those who are "information rich," with ready access to information communication technologies and networks, and those who do not have such access, the "information poor." Within Western society there is the expectation that technology, especially information technology, is not just something added to everyday life but an expected necessity or even a human right. Whether studying, working, shopping, socializing, or dealing with providers of essential services and government departments, Westerners are hard-pressed to function without some sort of investment, both financial and ideological, in technology. Nevertheless, access to this technology and its related educational and vocational opportunities is not uniform. Poverty, debt, and other forms of disadvantage result in an "information poverty" that removes the voices of some from the everyday conversations of society and church. For some, digital technologies prove to be barriers to entering into full participation in society, displacing people to the borderlands and muting their voices. Still others are removed from participation by the introduction of new technologies that turn them into a kind of refugee, also having to exist on the margins of a society that sees their skills or knowledge as redundant within the new digital world.

Who are the digitally displaced and digital refugees existing in the borderlands of our techno-cultural societies? Typically, they are those with lower incomes, people with low or no qualifications, single parents, the unemployed or underemployed, those in areas without a sound telecommunications infrastructure, ethnic minorities, and aged people. When you look at that list of people struggling in a digital society, you may be struck with how very similar it looks to the call throughout the Bible for the people of God to care for widows, orphans, tenants, the poor, resident aliens, and immigrant workers found within their midst (e.g., Deut. 10:12–19). The digitally displaced or digital refugees have become aliens within their own society. The call to the people of God to do justice and proclaim good news for the poor surely embraces a concern for those who are the information poor.

Both the church community and individuals are called to challenge practices, policies, and technologies that disenfranchise individuals and communities. Furthermore, they are called to assist those communities and individuals who suffer from information poverty, seeking to address its underlying causes and offering constructive aid to those suffering from it. It is critical that this be seen as a problem relating not just to society outside the church but also to whatever technological ventures the local and global church is pursuing. The question "What are we trying to do?" must be critiqued by the question "Whom does our approach exclude?" There is a very real danger that the effort to reach and serve others through the use of digital technology can create "gated" virtual communities that further marginalize those the church is especially called to speak for. Awareness of these silenced "virtual voices" within society opens up possibilities for creative ways that the church might engage with wider society. An example of this engagement with issues of social justice in relation to communications and media is the World Association for Christian Communication (WACC). A nongovernmental organization, WACC works from the standpoint that effective and accessible communications are essential for human dignity and flourishing communities. As such, the organization works internationally in an advocacy role and supports communications projects that promote social justice.[33]

How can you do this personally? In a Christian ministry or outreach context, you might consider that digital technologies and media provide an essential opportunity to enrich personal and community faith and relationships. This might mean developing digital resources for communicating information about the church community, such as a website posting service times, offering podcasts of previous sermons, providing devotional resources, maintaining pastoral care connections, or sharing prayer concerns. As part of that work, you may help set up a social media group for your church's youth program, because it seems like an appropriate forum for communicating with the members of that group. A good question to ask when doing that is not only who will this include but also what potential does this have for marginalizing some of those you are trying to support? While a social media group may be a good way to connect with the young people in this group, some may be left out because they are too young to legally have an account on the social media platform chosen or their parents or caregivers will not allow it. Moreover, it may favor those who have access to better technology for a variety of circumstances and push others to the margins of the community being built and maintained. It is not that use of social media is a bad thing in this context, but its use needs to be carefully considered and other actions taken to ensure that it does not exclude people from the community.

In a pastoral or leadership context, churches might work to support existing community programs or develop new ones that help those who are struggling with information technology, thereby empowering individuals and communities to participate more fully in the digital society around them. Examples of this might be teaching core information technology skills or helping people access information from social agencies or government departments via the internet. At a more basic level, something as simple as assisting with reading, writing, and numeracy in the local communities and schools can be impactful.[34]

Political and social engagement with businesses, educational establishments, and local and national government is another level of technology and media that Christians might engage. Here it is essential to help the voices of those marginalized by digital technologies to be heard. Critical reflection with these silenced voices will help to identify values communicated within the context of our technological cultures that reinforce the differences between information rich and poor.[35]

Another justice issue that is a by-product of our technological age is increased surveillance in society. This connects to previous discussions of publicized privacy, where our once-private actions and information are increasingly public. Surveillance ranges from the increased number of cameras recording our movements in public spaces to the tracking of people's online behaviors and sites visited through cookies for marketing purposes to the recording of our social media practices by government agencies concerned about global security issues. This creates collections of vast amounts of personal and communal data held by public entities and in online databases. These practices demand theological reflection by Christians about their appropriateness and contribution to both justice and well-being. In developing a Christian ethic of surveillance, including the notion that some forms of surveillance are necessary for certain forms of individual freedom and communal well-being, Eric Stoddart contends that truthfulness is the core value needed.[36] This truthfulness is developed from a biblical understanding of the need for integrity in human relationships and the dignity of the human person; thus surveillance must be both accurate and appropriate not only in the collection and content of data but also in its interpretation. For Stoddart, we preserve that human dignity through the control of our own personal data or the ability to monitor its use. Moreover, we have a mutual responsibility to see that our neighbor's personal data is maintained in the same way, and failure to do that diminishes not just their dignity as persons-in-relationship but also our own dignity.

While we might think this kind of engagement with public life has to do primarily with the state and corporate business, it has parallels within the communal life of the church. How we handle the personal information of those in our church communities falls under this ethic of truthfulness related to accurate and appropriate data collection. We must consider how to display people's phone numbers and email addresses, how we use images of members in church websites and magazines without permission, and how we publish membership numbers. Church members should be assured that their personal data is maintained with integrity, be able to check the content and how it is used, and function with the understanding that personal data will not be used for purposes they have not agreed to.

Finally, opportunities arise for the church and its members to model what living faithfully in a digital society looks like. Pastor and practical theologian Steve Taylor's idea of the postmodern monastery is one example of this. Here individuals who are fully conversant with the language and nature of the digital world seek to live a life that uses those skills creatively and justly through a deep awareness of the rhythms of prayer, grace, and service to God.[37] These "postmodern monks" form a community that is connected not only by virtual spaces but also by physical ones, creating shared daily spirituality that mixes both virtual and physical. In Taylor's vision these spaces exist

> as ethical communities, which could profoundly shape participants' spiritual development through prayer. Through the use of their technical skills to teach the digitally illiterate, postmodern monks can express the justice of God. By focusing their creativity, they offer the chance to develop quality spiritual products—"downloads"—among the pegging world of the Internet. Our contemporary technologies offer the missional opportunity for the creatively gifted to pass on the life-giving texts of Christianity.[38]

Identifying what is appropriate and ethical to the community they are seeking to engage, these creators identify the "pegs," or particular points of shared interest or experience in the online world, and innovatively deliver digital products that encourage people's spiritual and overall well-being. This comes back to an ethical imperative to appropriate technology that looks for ways in which God-given human creativity might be used to create and nurture well-being and to maintain and develop relationships from a deep-centered understanding of both who our neighbors are and how we might love them in the digital neighborhood. This integrity in relationships is picked up in the call to do kindness.

Acting with Mercy and Kindness in Our Digital World

In the previous section we reflected on the call to do justice in the digital world as well as on issues of neighborliness and use of or access to appropriate media and technology to address issues of marginalization, sustainability, and human creativity. Now we turn to the second strand of Micah's imperative, the call to love mercy, and how that might be lived out in our digital environments. Previously we noted that this manifestation of kindness as mercy reflects the way that God is faithful in his mercy and kindness (*hesed*) toward the world and all in it, going beyond charity and compassion to those in need and embracing a fullness of relationships that are marked by grace, generosity, and loyalty toward God and others. How then might this aspect of life, this *hesed*, with its strong relational aspect of loyalty, faithfulness, and steadfast love, with its movement toward *shalom* and well-being, be displayed in our digital lives?

One pathway into thinking about this is the concept of friendship, something that pastoral theologian Lynne Baab highlights in her book *Friending*, which examines the nature of relationships online.[39] Baab's approach is rooted in pastoral rather than philosophical concerns, and a dominant theme that runs through her book is that our starting point for looking at relationships in an online context is not the technology that mediates those relationships but rather what we think the content of wholesome relationships looks like. Noting that the word "friend" is transformed from a noun into a verb in the social network context, with the ideas of "friending" and "unfriending" people online, Baab draws out a theological portrait of friendship that is made up of both core virtues and related actions of intentionality and commitment. The biblical perspectives on these virtues and actions are located in the New Testament texts of 1 Corinthians 13 and Colossians 3, which themselves reflect the concept of *hesed*.

In 1 Corinthians 13, especially verses 4–8, Baab sees a definition of love that sits at the heart of true friendship. In one sense this description of love represents treating love as a noun, with themes of loyalty, affection, respect, sympathy, empathy, and understanding. These themes connect to traditional understandings of friendship, including companionship, affirmation, and acceptance. These virtues or aspects of love connect with shared values, interests, and experiences found in friendships and raise the question of how these kinds of friendships can be created, nurtured, and maintained. The answer to that question, Baab says, can be found in the Colossians 3 text, where "love" moves from being a noun to being a verb, something expressed in action. Thus, the actions of compassion, kindness, humility, meekness, patience, forbearance, and forgiveness found in verses 12–13 become the way in which life is organized, not only in the physical world, but also in the virtual ones we inhabit.

Baab identifies three key ways that digital media and communication assist friendship. First, social media allows people to connect, and reconnect, with family and others from their past and across ages and locations; this can play a role in restoring and reinforcing those relationships. Second, online media such as social networking, blogs, and photo sharing allow friendships to develop around shared interests. Third, we need to be mindful of using the appropriate technology and media for supporting friendships. In this case, Baab sees both physical and nonphysical presence as having positive and negative dimensions. She argues that while physical presence gives the fullness of multisensory encounter, the absence of physical presence can allow particular aspects of communication—for example, a voice on the phone or a written message—to be received more fully and deeply. Reflecting on this, she says:

> Most people still give priority to seeing their friends in person. In most cases, for most people, electronic means of communication sustain and nurture relationships until the pleasure of a face-to-face visit is possible. Text messages, emails, instant messages, Skype, and social networking can, with intentionality and care, be used to convey love and affection, and they can provide the opportunity for genuine sharing of emotions and concerns.[40]

Our digital practice calls us to reflect on not only the nature of our friendships in a digital age but also how we see and treat the other in digitally mediated contexts.

Practical theologian Pete Ward provides an example of acting with kindness in our networked relationships within Christian community. Ward describes the potential development of pastoral and spiritual networks supported by networked technologies, and in particular by text messaging. Although people in Christian community may meet face-to-face regularly or semi-regularly, the text message network can become a significant communication channel between the people in the group, a kind of communal glue. In this network, day-to-day comments on the experiences of life might be manifested in a way not possible in the physical meetings of the community.[41] While Ward is writing about text messaging here, the same immediacy of expression and response might also be found in the use of social networks such as Twitter and Facebook, or through email and blog networks, though at a slower pace.[42] For example, Tim Hutchings notes the development of midweek online "LifeGroups," part of the online and broadcast media Life Church network in the United States. Church participants can connect online to the church services and other online material and also interact in regular discipleship and fellowship groups in an online medium.[43]

It is important to note that in the cases of text messaging and online groups, the context they occur in shapes their form, and vice versa. The text message networks support the pastoral connections within a community, people who know each other in flesh-and-blood relationships. The constraints of the text message network mean that messages tend to be short and perhaps frequent, but these can be expanded on in face-to-face encounters at a later date. Reciprocally, the gaps between face-to-face encounters do not have to be spaces empty of communication, with text messages and other forms of digital communication strengthening the flesh-and-blood relationships between individuals and a wider group. Moreover, just as we have to work at and learn how to develop and support friendships and manifest faithful kindness and concern in physical encounters, so we need to learn and develop equivalent forms of social skills and etiquette in the digital spaces to be effective in doing that in both short- and long-term relationships.

Related to the development of those social skills and etiquette is discernment about how media technologies enable some people to develop and enhance relationships but do not do the same for others. As Baab notes, in the digital age we have access to a wide range of communication modes, which requires us to make informed decisions about which modes will work best for which relationships. Again, we must decide what we want the content of the relationship to be rather than first deciding on the technology we use. Not everyone responds well to or wants to use the same media contexts, and tensions can arise from the rapid and continual development of communications media, sometimes rendering preferred modes of communication obsolete or unsupported.

Prioritizing the content and ongoing trajectory of relationships shifts the focus from the mere use of technology toward emphasizing the human subjects within the relationship. We must pay attention to the human dimensions of the friendship as we consider how the relationship is to be initiated, maintained, and nurtured. This means reflecting on the way we use technology to serve both the personal dimension of the relationship and the purpose of the friendship. A friendship developed through shared interests and experiences can be quite different from one that develops out of an expression of care for another person, though both dimensions are often present. In all of this the questions around media and communications technologies return to the notion of who and where my neighbor is and how I treat my neighbor in ways that are authentic, loving, and just. Baab's approach to drawing on love as both a noun and a verb for underpinning those relationships goes deep into the nature of *hesed* and *shalom* in online environments, regardless of whom we encounter.

This concern with friendship is a significant strand running through the call to love mercy and kindness in digital worlds, but it is just one strand. The danger with a focus on friendship, even though rooted in love, is that it can become overly individualized and self-serving. It can place focus on *my* friendships, what function those friendships have for me, and how I am supported in everyday life by digital media and technologies. Baab's work does not go down that path, but the potential is there for friendship in itself to become an idol. For example, the perception of my own self-worth might be tied to the number of people who have accepted my social media friend requests or the number of people who respond to me through comments in social media or blogs. The primary focus is not the content of those "friendships" but rather some acknowledgment of my presence in the world by others. Returning to our definition of appropriate technology being economically productive, ecologically sound, socially just, and personally fulfilling, we would ask whether media technologies connect to personal fulfillment in a wholesome way. Moreover, our reflection on kindness and mercy and *shalom* supports not only individual well-being but also communal well-being brought about by integrity in relationships with both God and others. Therefore, we would add to the criteria of social justice and personal fulfillment the additional criterion of spiritual nourishment, which combines with these to promote integrity in relationships.

The Amish in North America are an example of a community that has developed its own perspective on what economic productivity, ecological soundness, social justice, personal fulfillment, and spiritual nourishment look like in relation to technology. According to Bill McKibben, the Amish community demonstrates a strong ethic of appropriate technology, which takes into account how particular technologies affect their community life. The Amish evaluate the appropriateness of a technology for their community with the criterion of whether the technology enhances or diminishes communal life and values. For example, they recognize the usefulness of telephones in emergencies, but they see technologies focused on individual communication as potentially disruptive to family life and rhythms, and so telephones are placed outside the home where the community can access them in cases of emergency. For McKibben, the Amish offer us one example that technological discernment is possible.[44]

Yet lifting up the Amish as exemplars of ethical technological use can be prone to simplistic understandings of such negotiations. Or, as Kevin Miller asserts, it can reduce our understanding about the impact of technologies on culture to either romanticized ideals or a hopelessly compromised position.[45]

A better way to do this, Miller contends, is not just to imitate what the Amish or similar conservative and bounded communities have done but rather to examine and weigh the principles and criteria used by these communities and to learn from them to critically recontextualize our own media choices in everyday life. Miller also points out that, while we might talk about "the Amish," there is significant diversity within Amish communities regarding what is or is not considered appropriate technology in light of their community values. This discernment varies across history, geography, and the relations particular Amish communities have with non-Amish society.

Nevertheless, Miller notes that across Amish and other Mennonite communities there is a common practice of discernment and understanding around technology and media that is "grounded in an ecclesiology structured to produce full accountability between individual members of the church and the will and discernment of the larger group."[46] In this there is some sort of communitarian decision making that reflects aspects of doing justice, loving mercy, and walking humbly with God.

For Miller, one of the key aspects in negotiating technology is how we think about time and the way it shapes our everyday life. Miller's conjecture is that we tend to focus on a more instrumental view of time (*chronos*), which allows us to order, manage, and control the world, rather than a more relational view of time (*kairos*) that comprises moments of meaning within a narrative of life. It is this relational view of time, seen in the New Testament (e.g., Gal. 4:4; Titus 1:1–3) to represent defining moments in history, that is captured in the approach to appropriate technology. Rather than concentrating on managing time and relationships, we should work on using and applying technology to create meaning and true relationships in our individual and communal lives. In this respect, the Amish community's approach to technology is connected to an experience or notion of time that serves the community rather than the other way around. Summarizing this, Miller says, "Spiritually we realize that the less *kairos* wholeness that we experience in our relationships and schedules and the more we are in tutelage to the god *chronos* (and its cousin mammon), the more our life stories feel plot-less, which is to say, pointless."[47] This differentiation of time and meaning-making is something that we will return to later in the context of worship.

In relation to the Amish approach to appropriate technology, Miller asserts that the relational values held communally provide a nuanced understanding of technological use. Values such as the significance of home and family life; the nurturing of relationships that are local, enduring, and stable; not being enslaved to a plurality of choices; and resisting individualism all contribute to this. Thus, the use of technology such as a mobile phone is weighed against how it would impact home life: Would it contribute to authentic and sustainable human relationships? Would it lead to an incessant need to have the next best thing? Would it privilege the individual over against the community? While such questions may seem at odds with the contemporary culture of infinite choice, instant gratification, and a fast-paced life, which many of us occupy, they provide an example of working out how technology might help, hinder, or sustain community and human relationships. The Amish community holds to certain beliefs about technology and its use: the community rather than individuals makes technological decisions; technology is not necessarily evil, so it can be used with caution; and the use of technology can potentially undermine the community and its core values.[48] This approach to appropriate technology is determined by a very clear sense of neighbors, neighborhood, and the significance of loyalty and fidelity to others, all of which provide a narrative of meaning to technological life in these communities.

The Amish illustration focuses on what an entire community might look like if it approached technology and media use through a communitarian lens. But what about individual choices for those living in the wider contemporary media culture? A reasonably simple, but at the same time significant, example relates to the choices we make about technology and transport. The What Would Jesus Drive? campaign run by the Evangelical Environmental Network in the United States asks what appropriate technology might be with respect to our personal transportation choices. With their belief that what we do to the environment and to each other matters to Jesus Christ, Lord of all creation, this group sees the choices that individuals and communities make about transportation as having a moral dimension. The effects of pollution on public health and environmental sustainability, dependence on imported oil, and the sourcing of that oil in relation to issues of peace and security feature in their consideration of transportation decisions. Their question does not demand a simple response like an electric car, a minivan, or a bus. Rather, it asks Christians to consider how the choices they make individually and in shaping public policy contribute to a common good. Criteria such as economic productivity, ecological soundness, social justice, personal fulfillment, and spiritual nourishment all come into that decision-making process.[49]

While we do not have to embrace all of the above assumptions, it is good to think about our own assumptions about technology, individually and communally, and examine how they may shape how we treat and use technology and media. While we may believe we use technology in ways that we consider kind and compassionate and that contribute to others' well-being, it is vital to look at or revisit the values that underpin those choices. We do this not only so that we "walk the talk" in acting justly, faithfully, and lovingly but also so that we remain walking humbly with God.

Walking Humbly with God and Technology

The preceding sections detail how our relationship with God in the digital and technological environments is manifested in our relationships with our neighbors in both the physical and the digital world. Here we take up the theme of walking humbly with God, particularly in the context of the worshiping Christian community. This includes recognition of our dependence on God for all things, authenticity in our relationship with God, and trusting God first before our own human ingenuity.

The act of Christian worship, of individuals and communities seeking to glorify God through responses of praise, thanksgiving, testimony, repentance, prayer, and often music, lies toward the heart of the Christian life. Through worship, believers respond to the reality of God in their lives and the world around them and are formed in the process. Ideally, this formation takes place as believers are nurtured spiritually, seek to discern God's will in their lives, are educated in the Christian faith, and encounter Scripture. The act of gathering to worship as a community forms both personal and communal identity, which in turn reflects both the unity and the diversity of the body of Christ, the church. For many, communal worship is the defining mark of their faith, while for others worship is a much more individual act by choice or by necessity. In any context, the ultimate purpose is to worship God in spirit and in truth (John 4:23–24).

This activity of worshiping God—Father, Son, and Holy Spirit—has been and continues to be intricately linked to technology and media. Examples include the construction of sites of worship such as cathedrals; the development of written texts such as the Bible or prayer books; and the use of music and various objects such as candles, incense, and particular clothing for ministers and others. More recently, we can add projector screens, audiovisual material, computer software, websites, computer applications, and mobile phones, all of which seek to add to the life of the believer in worship. Moreover, the technological environment we inhabit shapes the way we worship and the way we behave in the context of worship and the Christian life.

A Humble Approach to Technology

Reflecting on the technological environment we live in and the impact that it has on our Christian worship, Susan White argues that being immersed in such an environment has significant consequences. These consequences derive, she thinks, from the technological and media environments creating a level of dependency on technology for satisfying short-term needs.[50] Although White wrote this twenty or so years ago, the continual development of digital and media technologies has continued this trend, whether it's people phoning you because you did not reply immediately to their email or text message, or being upset if the book or movie you order online is not instantly delivered to you. White believes this kind of environment creates an expectation within the church that spiritual needs can be met in the same way—quickly, professionally, and with little personal effort. This is, in effect, a form of spiritual consumerism that can reduce spiritual practices and life to a question of whether there's an app for it.

It also reflects a shift in some church cultures toward professionalized ministry, so that ministry leaders are seen as service providers and worshipers are seen as spiritual consumers. The impact of media and technology can create a perception that meaningful participation in church life is reduced to those who are paid to do that in the context of pastoring, music, mission, and other ministries. Steve Taylor calls this "spiritual tourism," reflecting the wide range of motivations for people coming into the church community, some with the desire to consume and others with a desire to go beyond that.[51] How, then, do you provide spiritual food for palettes that have developed a taste for consuming things in bite-sized packages? Taylor's answer is to create resources and experiences that satisfy that palette ("spiritual takeout") but also draw it on to want something that is more substantial and takes longer to "eat."

Walking humbly with God is a lifelong journey, and many of the spiritual exercises, disciplines, and realities of the Christian life do not deliver everything instantly with little or no effort. One strand of appropriate media and technology in our worship and church communities is therefore to recognize people's short-term expectations and *chronos*-centered lives—to use Kevin Miller's terminology—and then assist and encourage them to deepen their walks with God by helping them to develop a longer view of time. As we commit to being with them on the journey, we can help them recognize when their desire for instant gratification has become an idol drawing their worship away from God.

At another level, an appropriate or humble approach to technology involves helping people develop skills to understand the cultural forces, such as technology and media, shaping their lives and faith and teaching them how to evaluate those forces in light of the gospel. Biblical scholar Kevin Vanhoozer observes that culture has a variety of dimensions that make this kind of analysis essential for wise living in the everyday world.[52] He notes that culture communicates not only information but also interpretations of that information, and in doing that it provides interpretative narratives with the power to orient individuals and communities in the world. Thus, culture provides us with both information and worldview that shape our thinking about our context and ourselves, as well as how we feel about those things. Moreover, it influences our understanding of right and wrong, and in doing that it shapes the very environment we create to live in. Culture, though, is not static or limited to a single location, because it reproduces or transmits beliefs, values, and practices from one social group to another, adding those to the environment in which we exist. All of this information—values, narratives, and worldviews—is transmitted and reproduced in such a way as to shape the spirit of who we are and the character of our societies. Culture cultivates, forming the human spirit and providing the soil and nutrients for flourishing or, in some cases, stunting growth. So a key component of appropriate technology and media is the examination of the cultures we live in and are creating, and evaluating how they affect how we walk humbly with God.

For example, in considering how mobile devices might frame Christian religious experience in relation to the production, consumption, and distribution of religious media texts, Ryan Torma and Paul Emerson Teusner drew the following conclusions. They observed that for a text to have meaning for those receiving it, it needed to respond to being "touched" and manipulated. The expected aesthetics for a mobile device, mediated by the media culture the device user is situated in, meant that the religious text, such as a biblical passage, liturgy, or sermon, needed to behave and respond according to those expectations in order to be meaningful. The small amount of text displayed on the relatively small screens needed to be supplemented by audiovisual aids or textual cues that promoted movement through the text. Additionally, the text needed to behave according to the expected interactions of a mobile device, providing rapid feedback to users when touched, and also be able to be manipulated for reflection and sharing online with others.[53] This highlights how the media culture of the day shapes the meaning attributed to aspects of the Christian faith, such as religious texts, by whether the form they are encountered in meets the expectations of that culture, regardless of any other authority vested in them. Those working with media culture and its artifacts need to be aware of these kinds of influences so that the production of media and use of technology are faithful and will be well received.

Co-creating Humbly with God

As noted earlier in this book, human creative agency is intimately tied to digital media, both in the creation of that technology and in the way it is used and appropriated. An increasingly common way to talk theologically about human beings' creativity, particularly with respect to technology, is to use the language of co-creation. Sometimes this language is used simply to assert that by virtue of being made in the image of a creator God, we are innately creative. At a deeper level, however, it represents the idea that the body of Christ can create together in innovative ways, particularly in church and worship contexts, to enable greater participation by church members within the life of the church.[54]

The description of human beings as "created co-creators," promoted particularly by Lutheran theologian Philip Hefner, has proven influential in the engagement of science and religion and for examining human technological agency.[55] The "created" aspect of the description alerts us to the fact that human beings are physically embodied creatures who must see themselves as created, dependent, and finite. In doing that, human beings recognize they are fundamentally different from God, their creator. The second aspect, "co-creator," speaks of a human calling or vocation to act as a creative agent within the natural world. For Hefner, God has produced humanity to be part of the purposeful creative process in the cosmos and to partner with God in that. Furthermore, the creative activity of God in the world embraces both *creatio ex nihilo* (creation out of nothing) and *creatio continua* (ongoing creation): the God who created the universe continues God's creative agency through that universe's history. In practical terms, this means that human beings are called to create wisely and creatively in the world, including in the areas of digital technology and media. Furthermore, we are to do so in a way that is guided by loving action, with justice and mercy and a humility that all creative action is ultimately sourced in and dependent upon God. Human creativity that is done with integrity and wisdom and creates well-being is to be celebrated and enjoyed; human creativity that damages relationships and the environment, oppresses and dehumanizes others, and fails to recognize the lordship of God in creation is to be challenged and avoided.

Over the past few years, in the weeks leading up to Easter, Presbyterian Youth Ministries (PYM) in New Zealand has experimented with using text messaging and social media to narrate the biblical accounts of Easter.[56] Working on the principle that the biblical accounts have always been contextualized in some form, PYM presented the narratives in a form suitable for those media channels. The aim was to remain faithful to the story being told while respecting the context of the media channels used without costing their target audience of young people financially. People opted in to the "Kiwi Easter" text messaging, Facebook, or Twitter feeds, and over the period of Holy Week received messages that narrated the Easter accounts. Messages were short, snappy, and colloquial, as if being tweeted from the perspective of an eyewitness, such as Peter following Jesus. This simple venture was well received by the wider public and covered in the news media. It was adapted and updated each year with a different focus and led to the production of a "Kiwi Advent" version of the text messaging system.[57] The presentation took into account the economic and social dimensions in its format and channels, contributed to community discussion and participation around the celebration of Easter, and looked to spiritually nourish those who participated. As such, it could be described as an example of appropriate use of technology and media.

Those who are pessimistic about technology tend to emphasize the dimension of human finitude and limitedness, particularly connected to human sinfulness and self-interest. The optimists stress the potential in technology for good, technology as a divine vocation, and have a more favorable view of human beings. Interpreting the image-bearing human being as the created co-creator shaped by the imperatives to do justice, love mercy, and walk humbly with God allows both pessimism and optimism to be redirected into a hopeful narrative. Theologically, human beings can understand themselves as creators of technology and media because they bear the *imago Dei*. The drive to act purposefully and creatively in the world is born out of a vocation given by God to represent God humbly in the world and act within that world on God's behalf.[58]

Honesty and Authenticity with Technology before God

The final strand of walking humbly with God that we will take up here is the way in which technology and media might be used as an avenue for expressing an individual's or community's relationship with God. The potential for Christians to become critical, discerning consumers and producers of digital technologies and media opens the door for a variety of religious expressions in online environments. Whether on Facebook or Twitter or through blogging, collaborative work using wikis or Google Docs, image and video sharing on Flickr or YouTube, or basic email and text messaging, there are ample opportunities to respond to individual and community faith contexts in public and private settings. With online connectivity, easy-to-use tools for the creation of online content, and cheap online storage now commonplace, people are able to access not just their traditional faith resources but also a much broader range of spiritual traditions and teaching, allowing them to discover the variety of expressions and spiritual practices within the breadth and history of Christianity. Digital technologies and media also allow individuals and communities to experiment with new forms or traditions in the online environment.

One example of this experimentation is the way traditional religious practices involving labyrinths have made the transition into the online world. In Christian spirituality, the labyrinth is a physical, mazelike pathway you follow from the outside to the center and back out again. Labyrinths can be inside a building, such as the labyrinth in Chartres Cathedral in France, or outside, marked with paving and paths, or even be created temporarily at a location, say by mowing a pattern into a lawn or laying out a pattern with rope. Walking through a labyrinth connects to the theme of pilgrimage, moving from the outside toward God and then back to the world again. This idea of pilgrimage has made its way into online spaces—from mobile device applications that act as travel guides and prayer diaries on pilgrimage trails such as the Camino de Santiago, to online pilgrimages in environments such as Second Life and web-based labyrinth experiences. One of the earliest and still-existent instances of the latter is the online labyrinth website born out of the use of physical labyrinths in worship by various British alternative worship communities in the late 1990s and early 2000s.[59] The online site invites users to enter into a series of meditative exercises drawing the user in toward God and then back out to the world. The virtual replication of the physical labyrinth experience is created through the use of music, audio effects, narration, and visual elements. While now almost fifteen years old, it continues to function well.

The online labyrinth recovers a particular religious tradition and practice and brings it into the online space. Another practice that might be recovered in a similar way is the tradition of lament within the Christian community. Lament is not a particularly common topic talked about in churches, though it is the dominant type of psalm in the Bible. Some, such as Carl Trueman, think this is because the Christian church in the Western world, and especially the evangelical church, has bought into a gospel of health, wealth, and happiness, focusing on positive hymns and songs that fail to recognize the negative dimensions of the human condition.[60] This, he claims, is a theologically and pastorally dangerous scenario in a world of broken people, and he raises the challenge to the church to reclaim the language of lament in worship so those who are suffering, lonely, and dispossessed do not lose their voices inside the church.

New media allow both the emergence of new forms of discourse and forums for more traditional expression. Presentations of lament might include traditional biblical psalms of lament being performed on YouTube, perhaps with the addition of background music or visual imagery, or preached about in a local context but made available via the internet. Alternatively, original psalms of lament and complaint might be performed or presented in new media formats, often mixing material from various sources into a final media product.

Lament is also explored through new media in the contexts of education and counseling. Mark Roncace and Patrick Gray describe how they explore the genre of psalms of lament and imprecation (curse) by having students engage with popular culture and digital technology. Students are asked to seek out aspects within those media that reflect the phase of disorientation noted by biblical scholar Walter Brueggemann and to identify ways in which those media help or hinder the move to a new orientation of well-being.[61] The role of lament is also explored online through groups providing educational and spiritual resources for social workers or counselors or for those seeking a way of expressing their current experiences.[62] In each of these cases, we see the intersection between lament, the internet, and digital media developing in intriguing ways.

Similarly, those seeking to understand how worship might take place within a culture saturated in new media are also carrying out experiments in this area. For instance, United Kingdom musician, blogger, and "worship curator" Jonny Baker explains how lament was incorporated into the life of his London community of faith. Paying particular attention to lament, Baker mixed the tradition of the psalms in worship with contemporary video material to draw the congregation into creating their own psalms relating to their particular contexts. After the event, moving from more traditional, static forms of media into the new media environment, Baker used his blog to communicate what happened, link to resources used, and encourage feedback from others (via the blog) on the ideas presented there.[63]

With their power to enhance communication and participation, digital technologies offer new spaces for lament as well as thanksgiving and worship. Moreover, new media offer possibilities for much-needed lament to occur in spaces that perhaps have been eliminated from traditional worshiping communities, serving to critique the lack of space within churches for lament as a worship practice. An instance of creating space for lament in a new media environment occurred in late 2010. In November of that year, the deaths of twenty-nine miners in a mine accident on the west coast of New Zealand created a deep sense of national mourning, generating a variety of lamentations and other responses. The band U2 was touring New Zealand at that time, and their concerts provided a space for that public grief and lament to be expressed. Through the combination of lead singer Bono's short reflection on the tragedy, the performance of "One Tree Hill" (a song about loss with New Zealand connections), and the projection of the names of lost miners on video screens, the band created a space where the audience could share in and express the rawness and grief that affected the nation at that time.

What moved the U2 concert space into a form of new media lament was a combination of mainstream media and the use of new media to communicate that experience to the wider public.[64] Video clips of U2's engagement with the tragedy were recorded on mobile devices and uploaded to sites like Facebook and YouTube with comments from both posters and viewers.[65] Though not all comments were relevant, messages of sympathy, additional lament, and a sense of being part of the community caught up in the tragedy were communicated, and links to the clips and comments were passed on to friends and others. Explicit theological, pastoral, and personal reflection about the tragedy also took place on news sites and blogs. Theologian Steve Taylor used his blog to write a piece, "U2 and Public Lament for Pike River Miners," that explored the connection between the concert and lament in general, while also providing links to others writing on similar themes. Readers of Taylor's material took advantage of the space to comment.[66] Taylor, together with biblical scholar Liz Boase, later followed this up with further reflection on the public role of lament in the Australian context of bushfires.[67] Similarly, the mainstream media made space for the wider public to express their feelings about the tragedy, with newspaper websites posting condolences and sentiments from the New Zealand public and those farther afield.

The discussion above shows how new media can provide an appropriate and supportive environment to allow the experience of tragedy and trauma to be expressed in ways that help individuals and communities. Conversely, walking humbly with God through something like honest, appropriate lament can be lost if the power of this form of expression is misused or misapplied, either in online or physical contexts. Because lament is an act of performance, the commoditization of lament in a new media world, perhaps in the form of a service or mobile device application to be purchased, could lead to lament becoming a sanitized means to make money and feed spiritual narcissism. Lament should never become disconnected from the Easter hope of transformation offered through the life, death, and resurrection of Jesus Christ, not necessarily in a mobile app that claims to bring that, but rather in the fullness of a new orientation arising from being in Christ and from the future hope offered in God.

Conclusion

This chapter, here at the end of the book, has sketched out how we think a networked theology might be brought about through contemplating and enacting biblical and theological themes of justice, mercy, love of God and neighbor, and humility before God in connection to the media culture we find ourselves immersed in. We argue that this networked theology offers a distinct approach, which supports an appropriate technology that seeks to create *shalom* through a Christ-centered focus on technology and media—one that balances economic productivity with social justice and environmental sustainability with personal fulfillment and is spiritually nourishing to individuals and communities.

This networked theology involves a grappling of faith that seeks to understand our technological and media world and asks how we should live faithfully in that world as the people of God, the body of Christ, and the dwelling place of the Holy Spirit. This is not a theology or a way of life to be lived only within the confines of the church. Rather, networked theology is a public and contextual theology that engages with all aspects of our everyday world. It requires us to contemplate who we are, how we should live, and how we might encounter and engage others constructively and lovingly in our media culture. It does not shrink from our online and virtual worlds but recognizes the humanity of the people who are present there and the ongoing presence of God in both physical and virtual environments.

A networked theology requires that Christians think deeply about technology and media, and not just as tools to be used or put aside. We are, rather, to think about the values, inherent character, and environments created by technology and media as wider socio-technological systems. Networked theology confronts us with the question of what it means to love God and love neighbor in such a world. We are called by Christ to do both of these with all our being, and it is in our neighborhoods, physical or networked, that we encounter God and each other and follow these commands. The end goal of networked theology is to glorify Jesus Christ in God through the Holy Spirit. To do this we seek to establish communities of *shalom* that reflect true neighborliness through the recognition of others as persons and through integrity in all our relationships.

bibliography

Ahuja M. K., and K. M. Carley. "Network Structure in Virtual Organizations." *Journal of Computer-Mediated Communication* 3, no. 4 (1998). http://jcmc.indiana.edu/vol3/issue4/ahuja.html.

Ammerman, N. T. *Congregation and Community*. New Brunswick, NJ: Rutgers University Press, 1997.

Andrews, Dave. *Christi-Anarchy: Discovering a Radical Spirituality of Compassion*. Oxford: Lion, 1999.

Armfield, G. G., and R. L. Holbert. "The Relationship between Religiosity and Internet Use." *Journal of Media and Religion* 3, no. 2 (2003): 129–44.

Arthur, Chris, and World Association for Christian Communication. *Religion and the Media: An Introductory Reader*. Cardiff: University of Wales Press, 1993.

Baab, L. M. *Friending: Real Relationships in a Virtual World*. Downers Grove, IL: InterVarsity, 2011.

———. *Reaching Out in a Networked World: Expressing Your Congregation's Heart and Soul*. Herndon, VA: Alban Institute, 2008.

Bacon, F. "The New Organon." In *The Works of Francis Bacon*, vol. 4, edited by F. Bacon, J. Spedding, R. L. Ellis, and D. D. Heath, 39–248. London: Longman, 1857.

Baer, D. A., and R. P. Gordon. "Hesed." In *The New International Dictionary of Old Testament Theology and Exegesis*, edited by Willem VanGemeren, 211–18. Grand Rapids: Zondervan, 1997.

Bakardjieva, M. "Internet in Everyday Life: Exploring the Tenets and Contributions of Diverse Approaches." In *The Handbook of Internet Studies*, edited by C. Ess and M. Consalvo, 59–82. Oxford: Blackwell, 2011.

Barbour, I. G. *Ethics in an Age of Technology: The Gifford Lectures Volume 2*. San Francisco: HarperSanFrancisco, 1993.

Barker, E. "Crossing the Boundary: New Challenges to Religious Authority and Control as a Consequence of Access to the Internet." In *Religion and Cyberspace*, edited by M. Hojsgaard and M. Warburg, 67–85. London: Routledge, 2005.

Barna Research Group. "Cyber Church: Pastors and the Internet." Barna. February 11, 2015. www.barna.org/barna-update/congregations/706-cyber-church-pastors-and-the-internet#.VkvD2GSrSew.

Baym, N. K. "The Emergence of Community in Computer-Mediated Communication." In *CyberSociety*, edited by S. Jones, 138–63. Thousand Oaks, CA: Sage, 1995.

———. "The Emergence of On-Line Community." In *CyberSociety 2.0: Revisiting Computer-Mediated Community and Communication*, edited by S. G. Jones, 35–68. Thousand Oaks, CA: Sage, 1998.

Bednar, T. "Blogging: Report from a Grassroots Revival." *Stimulus* 12, no. 3 (2004): 24–30.

Beer, D., and R. Burrows. "Sociology and, of and in Web 2.0: Some Initial Considerations." *Sociological Research Online* 12, no. 5 (2007). www.socresonline.org.uk/12/5/17.html.

Beiler, Ryan. "Would Jesus Drive a Mercedes? The Untapped Potential of Biodiesel." *Sojourners Magazine* 35, no. 1 (2006). https://sojo.net/magazine/january-2006/would-jesus-drive-mercedes.

Bennett, R., and H. Campbell. "Modern-Day Martyrs: Fans' Online Reconstruction of Celebrities as Divine." In *Social Media, Religion and Spirituality*, edited by D. Herbert and M. Gillispe, 103–20. Berlin: De Gruyter, 2014.

Bevans, Stephen B. *Models of Contextual Theology*. Maryknoll, NY: Orbis Books, 2002.

Boase, Elizabeth, and Steve Taylor. "Lament in an Age of New Media." In *Spiritual Complaint: Theology and Practice of Lament*, edited by Miriam J. Bier and Tim Bulkeley, 205–27. Eugene, OR: Pickwick, 2013.

Bock, Darrell L. *Luke*. NIV Application Commentary. Grand Rapids: Zondervan, 1996.

Bonino, J. M. *Room to Be People: An Interpretation of the Message of the Bible for Today's World*. Translated by V. Leach. Geneva: World Council of Churches, 1975.

Brasher, B. *Give Me That Online Religion*. San Francisco: Jossey-Bass, 2001.

Brewin, K. *The Complex Christ: Signs of Emergence in the Urban Church*. London: SPCK, 2004.

Briggs, J. C. "Bacon's Science and Religion." In *The Cambridge Companion to Bacon*, edited by M. Peltonen, 172–99. Cambridge: Cambridge University Press, 1996.

Bruckman, A. "Identity Workshop: Emergent Social and Psychological Phenomena in Text-Based Virtual Reality." Unpublished paper, MIT Media Laboratory, 1992. http://www-static.cc.gatech.edu/~asb/papers.

Brueggemann, W. "Voices of the Night—Against Justice." In *To Act Justly, Love Tenderly, Walk Humbly: An Agenda for Ministers*, edited by W. Brueggemann, S. Daloz Parks, and T. H. Groome, 5–28. New York: Paulist Press, 1986.

Burkhalter, B. "Reading Race Online: Discovering Racial Identity in Usenet Discussions." In *Communities in Cyberspace*, edited by M. A. Smith and P. Kollock, 60–75. New York: Routledge, 1999.

Campbell, H. "Bloggers and Religious Authority Online." *Journal of Computer-Mediated Communication* 15, no. 2 (2010b): 251–76.

———. *Exploring Religious Community Online: We Are One in the Network*. New York: Peter Lang, 2005.

———. *An Investigation of the Nature of Church through an Analysis of Christian Email-Based Online Communities*. PhD diss., University of Edinburgh, 2001.

———. "Understanding the Relationship between Religious Practice Online and Offline in a Networked Society." *Journal of the American Academy of Religion* 80, no. 1 (2012): 64–93.

———. *When Religion Meets New Media*. London: Routledge, 2010.

Campbell, H., and M. Lövheim. "Studying the Online-Offline Connection in Religion Online." *Information, Communication & Society* 14, no. 8 (2011): 1083–96.

Careaga, A. *E-vangelism: Sharing the Gospel in Cyberspace*. Lafayette, LA: Huntington House, 1999.

Caritas Aotearoa New Zealand. *The Digital Divide: Poverty and Wealth in the Information Age*. Wellington: Caritas Aotearoa New Zealand, 2000.

Castells, Manuel. *The Rise of the Network Society*. Vol. 1 of *The Information Age: Economy, Society and Culture*. 2nd ed. Malden, MA: Blackwell, 2000.

Cheong, P. H., A. Halavais, and K. Kwon. "The Chronicles of Me: Understanding Blogging as a Religious Practice." *Journal of Media and Religion* 7, no. 3 (2008): 107–31.

Cheong, P. H., and J. P. H. Poon. "Weaving Webs of Faith: Examining Internet Use and Religious Communication among Chinese Protestant Transmigrants."

Journal of International and Intercultural Communication 2, no. 3 (2009): 189–207.

Clark, L. S. "Spirituality Online: Teen Friendship Circles and the Internet." Paper presented at The Fourth International Conference on Media, Religion and Culture, Louisville, September 1–4, 2004.

Clough, D. "The Message of the Medium: The Challenge of the Internet to the Church and Other Communities." *Studies in Christian Ethics* 13, no. 2 (2000): 91–100.

Cole-Turner, Ronald. *The New Genesis: Theology and the Genetic Revolution*. Louisville: Westminster John Knox, 1993.

———. "Science, Technology and Mission." In *The Local Church in a Global Era: Reflections for a New Century*, edited by M. L. Stackhouse, T. Dearborn, and S. Paeth, 100–112. Grand Rapids: Eerdmans, 2000.

———. "Science, Technology and the Mission of Theology in a New Century." In *God and Globalization*. Vol. 2, *The Spirit and the Modern Authorities*, edited by M. L. Stackhouse, and D. S. Browning, 139–65. Harrisburg, PA: Trinity Press International, 2001.

Crowley, E. D. *Liturgical Art for a Media Culture*. Collegeville, MN: Liturgical Press, 2007.

———. *A Moving Word: Media Art in Worship*. Minneapolis: Augsburg Fortress, 2006.

Darragh, Neil. *Doing Theology Ourselves: A Guide to Research and Action*. Auckland, NZ: Accent, 1995.

David, N. *Staying Safe Online*. Cambridge: Grove Books, 2007.

Dawson, L. L., and J. Hennebry. "New Religions and the Internet: Recruiting in a New Public Space." In *Religion Online—Finding Faith on the Internet*, edited by L. L. Dawson and D. E. Cowan, 151–73. New York: Routledge, 2004.

Elias, N., and D. Lemish. "Spinning the Web of Identity: The Roles of the Internet in the Lives of Immigrant Adolescents." *New Media & Society* 11, no. 4 (2009): 533–51.

Ellison, Katherine. "Stopping Traffic: What Would Jesus Drive?" *Christian Century* 119, no. 24 (2002). http://www.christiancentury.org/article/2002-11/stopping-traffic.

Ellul, J. *The Technological Society*. New York: Vintage Books, 1964.

Ess, C., and M. Consalvo. "Introduction: What Is Internet Studies?" In *The Handbook of Internet Studies*, edited by C. Ess and M. Consalvo, 1–8. Oxford: Blackwell, 2011.

Ferre, J. "The Media of Popular Piety." In *Mediating Religion: Conversation in Media, Religion and Culture*, edited by J. Mitchell and S. Marriage, 83–92. London: T&T Clark, 2003.

Ford, D. *Theology*. Oxford: Oxford University Press, 1999.

Forrester, D. B. *Christian Justice and Public Policy*. Cambridge: Cambridge University Press, 1997.

———. "The Scope of Public Theology." *Studies in Christian Ethics* 17, no. 2 (2004): 5–19.

———. "Social Justice and Welfare." In *The Cambridge Companion to Christian Ethics*, edited by R. Gill, 195–208. Cambridge: Cambridge University Press, 2002.

Friesen, D. J. *Thy Kingdom Connected: What the Church Can Learn from Facebook, the Internet, and Other Networks*. Grand Rapids: Baker Books, 2009.

Gardner, C. J. "Tangled in the Worst of the Web: What Internet Porn Did to One Pastor, His Wife, His Ministry, Their Life." *Christianity Today* 45, no. 4 (2001): 42–49.

Garner, S. "Image-Bearing Cyborgs?" *Interface* 15, no. 1 (2011): 31–50.

———. "Theology and the New Media." In *Digital Religion: Understanding Religious Practice in New Media Worlds*, edited by H. Campbell, 251–65. London: Routledge, 2013.

Gascoigne, Robert. *The Public Forum and Christian Ethics*. Cambridge: Cambridge University Press, 2001.

Gates, Bill. *The Road Ahead*. New York: Viking, 1995.

Graham, Elaine L., Heather Walton, and Frances Ward. *Theological Reflection: Methods*. London: SCM, 2005.

Grenz, Stanley J. *The Moral Quest: Foundations of Christian Ethics*. Leicester, UK: Apollos, 1997.

———. *The Social God and the Relational Self: A Trinitarian Theology of the Imago Dei*. Louisville: Westminster John Knox, 2001.

———. *Theology for the Community of God*. Carlisle: Paternoster, 1994.

Gryboski, Michael. "A Holographic Bible? Microsoft Technology Offers 'Intriguing' Way for Future Bible Study." *Christian Post*, January 28, 2015. www.christianpost.com/news/a-holographic-bible-microsoft-technology-offers-intriguing-way-for-future-bible-study-133235/.

Gutiérrez, G. *A Theology of Liberation*. Translated by S. C. Inda and J. Eagleson. London: SCM, 1974.

Hafner, Katie, and Matthew Lyon. *Where Wizards Stay Up Late: Origins of the Internet*. New York: Simon & Schuster, 1996.

Hall, D. J. *Professing the Faith: Christian Theology in a North American Context*. Minneapolis: Fortress, 1993.

Hall, T. Hartley, IV. "The Shape of Reformed Piety." In *Spiritual Traditions for the Contemporary Church*, edited by Robin Maas and Gabriel O'Donnell, 202–21. Nashville: Abingdon, 1990.

Hefner, P. *The Human Factor: Evolution, Culture and Religion*. Minneapolis: Fortress, 1993.

———. *Technology and Human Becoming*. Minneapolis: Fortress, 2003.

Helland, C. "Canadian Religious Diversity Online: A Network of Possibilities." In *Religion and Diversity in Canada*, edited by P. Beyer and L. Beaman, 127–48. Boston: Brill, 2008.

———. "Online-Religion/Religion-Online and Virtual Communitas." In *Religion on the Internet: Research Prospects and Promises*, edited by D. E. Cowan and J. K. Hadden, 205–23. New York: JAI, 2000.

Herring, D. "Virtual as Contextual: A Net News Theology." In *Religion Online*, edited by L. Dawson and D. Cowan, 149–65. New York: Routledge, 2005.

Hiebert, Paul G. "Conversion, Culture and Cognitive Categories." *Gospel in Context* 1, no. 4 (1978): 24–29.

Holt, S. C. *God Next Door: Spirituality and Mission in the Neighbourhood*. Brunswick East, Australia: Acorn Press, 2007.

Hoover, S. M. *Religion in the Media Age*. New York: Routledge, 2006.

Hopper, D. H. *Technology, Theology, and the Idea of Progress*. Louisville: Westminster John Knox, 1991.

Horsfield, P. G. "Media." In *Key Words in Religion, Media and Culture*, edited by D. Morgan, 111–22. New York: Routledge, 2008.

———. *The Mediated Spirit*. Commission for Mission, Uniting Church in Australia, Synod of Victoria, Melbourne, Australia, 2002. CD-ROM.

Horsfield, P. G., and K. Asamoah-Gyadu. "What Is It about the Book? Semantic and Material Dimensions in the Mediation of the Word of God." *Studies in World Christianity* 17, no. 2 (2011): 175–93.

Horsfield, P. G., and P. Teusner. "A Mediated Religion: Historical Perspectives on Christianity and the Internet." *Studies in World Christianity* 13, no. 3 (2007): 278–95.

Houston, G. *Virtual Morality: Christian Ethics in the Computer Age*. Leicester: Apollos, 1998.

Houtepen, A. *People of God: A Plea for the Church*. London: SCM, 1984.

Hutchings, T. "Creating Church Online: A Case-Study Approach to Religious Experience." *Studies in World Christianity* 13, no. 3 (2007): 243–60.

———. "Creating Church Online: Five Ethnographic Case Studies of Online Christian Community." PhD diss., Durham University, 2010.

Jacobs, S. "Virtually Sacred: The Performance of Asynchronous Cyber-Rituals in Online Spaces." *Journal of Computer-Mediated Communication* 12, no. 3 (2007). http://jcmc.indiana.edu/vol12/issue3/jacobs.html.

Jenkins, S. "Rituals and Pixels: Experiments in Online Church." *Online—Heidelberg Journal of Religions on the Internet* 3, no. 1 (2008). http://archiv.ub.uniheidelberg.de/volltextserver/volltexte/2008/8291/pdf/jenkins.pdf.

Jinkins, M. *Invitation to Theology: A Guide to Study, Conversation & Practice*. Downers Grove, IL: InterVarsity, 2001.

Jones, Steven G. "The Internet and Its Social Landscape." In *Virtual Culture: Identity and Communication in Cybersociety*, edited by Steven G. Jones, 7–35. Thousand Oaks, CA: Sage, 1997.

Katz, J., and R. Rice. *Social Consequences of Internet Use: Access Involvement and Interaction*. Cambridge, MA: MIT Press, 2002.

Kavanagh, A., and S. Patterson. "The Impact of Community Computer Networks on Social Capital and Community Involvement in Blacksburg." In *The Internet in Everyday Life*, edited by B. Wellman and C. Haythornthwaite, 325–44. Oxford: Blackwell, 2002.

Kelly, K. "Nerd Theology." *Technology in Society* 21, no. 4 (1999): 387–92.

———. "The Third Culture." *Science* 279 (1998): 992–93.

Kollock, P., and M. Smith. "Managing the Virtual Commons: Cooperation and Conflict in Computer Communities." In *Computer-Mediated Communication: Studies in Linguistic, Social, and Cross-Cultural Perspectives*, edited by Susan Herring, 110–28. Amsterdam: J. Benjamins, 1994.

Kraut, R., M. Patterson, V. Lundmark, S. Kiesler, T. Mukopadhyay, and W. Scherlis. "Internet Paradox: A Social Technology That Reduces Social Involvement and Psychological Well-Being?" *American Psychologist* 53 (1998): 1017–32.

Kraybill, D. B., S. M. Nolt, and D. Weaver-Zercher. *The Amish Way: Patient Faith in a Perilous World*. San Francisco: Jossey-Bass, 2010.

Krueger, O. "The Internet as a Mirror and Distributor of Religious and Ritual Knowledge." *Asian Journal of Social Sciences* 32, no. 2 (2004): 183–97.

Lövheim, M. *Intersecting Identities: Young People, Religion and Interaction on the Internet*. Uppsala, Sweden: Uppsala University, 2004.

Lövheim, M., and A. G. Linderman. "Constructing Religious Identity on the Internet." In *Religion and Cyberspace*, edited by M. Hojsgaard and M. Warburg. London: Routledge, 2005.

Lyon, D. "Would God Use Email?" *Zadok Perspectives* 71 (2001): 20–23.

MacKenzie, D., and J. Wajcman. *The Social Shaping of Technology: How the Refrigerator Got Its Hum*. 2nd ed. Milton Keynes, UK: Open University, 2001.

Manovich, Lev. *The Language of New Media*. Cambridge, MA: MIT Press, 2001.

———. "New Media from Borges to HTML." *The New Media Reader* (2003): 13–28.

Marshall, C. D. *Compassionate Justice: An Interdisciplinary Dialogue with Two Gospel Parables on Law, Crime, and Restorative Justice*. Eugene, OR: Cascade Books, 2012.

———. *Kingdom Come: The Kingdom of God in the Teaching of Jesus*. Auckland: Bible College of New Zealand, 1990.

———. "What Language Shall I Borrow? The Bilingual Dilemma of Public Theology." *Stimulus* 13, no. 3 (2005): 11–18.

McKibben, B. *Enough: Staying Human in an Engineered Age*. New York: Times Books, 2003.

McLuhan, M. *Understanding Media*. New York: Signet Books, 2001.

McMorris, Christine. "What Would Jesus Drive?" *Religion in the News* 6, no. 1 (2003): 19–21.

Meadows, P. R. "The Gospel in Cyberspace: Reflections on Virtual Reality." *Epworth Review* 22 (1995): 53–73.

Media 7. "Christian Media." Produced by Phil Wallington. TVNZ & Top Shelf Productions, 1999.

Meriwether, Lester. "35 Ways Your Church Can Promote Adult and Family Literacy in Your Community." *Texas Adult & Family Literacy Quarterly* 13, no. 2 (April 2009). http://www-tcall.tamu.edu/newsletr/apr09/apr09c.html.

Merritt, Jonathan. "Why Technology Didn't (and Won't) Destroy the Church." Religious News Service, February 27, 2015. http://jonathanmerritt.religionnews.com/2015/02/27/technology-hasnt-wont-destroy-church/.

Migliore, D. *Faith Seeking Understanding: An Introduction to Christian Theology*. 2nd ed. Grand Rapids: Eerdmans, 2004.

Miller, K. D. "Technological Prudence: What the Amish Can Teach Us." *Christian Reflection: A Series in Faith and Ethics* (2011): 20–28.

Mission and Public Affairs Council. *Mission-Shaped Church: Church Planting and Fresh Expressions of Church in a Changing Context*. London: Church House, 2004.

Mitcham, C., and J. Grote. "Aspects of Christian Exegesis: Hermeneutics, the Theological Virtues, and Technology." In *Theology and Technology: Essays in Christian Analysis and Exegesis*, edited by C. Mitcham and J. Grote, 21–24. Lanham, MD: University Press of America, 1984.

Monsma, S. V. *Responsible Technology: A Christian Perspective*. Grand Rapids: Eerdmans, 1986.

Moody, K. S. "Researching Theo(b)logy: Emerging Christian Communities and the Internet." In *Exploring Religion and the Sacred in a Media Age*, edited by C. Deacy and E. Arweck, 237–51. Farnham, UK: Ashgate, 2009.

Nardi, B. A., and V. O'Day. *Information Ecologies: Using Technology with Heart*. Cambridge, MA: MIT Press, 1999.

Newbigin, L. *Foolishness to the Greeks: The Gospel and Western Culture*. Grand Rapids: Eerdmans, 1986.

Niebuhr, H. R. *Christ and Culture*. New York: Harper, 1951.

Noble, D. F. *The Religion of Technology: The Divinity of Man and the Spirit of Invention*. New York: Alfred A. Knopf, 1997.

Nolland, J. *Luke 9:21–18:34*. Dallas: Word Books, 1993.

O'Leary, S., and B. Brasher. "The Unknown God of the Internet." In *Philosophical Perspectives on Computer-Mediated Communication*, edited by C. Ess, 233–69. Albany: State University of New York Press, 1996.

Ottmar, J. "Cyberethics: New Challenges or Old Problems." *Concilium* 1 (2005): 15–26.

Peters, Ted. *God—the World's Future: Systematic Theology for a New Era*. 2nd ed. Minneapolis: Fortress, 2000.

Pontifical Council for Social Communications. "The Church and Internet." Vatican, February 22, 2002. www.vatican.va/roman_curia/pontifical_councils/pccs/documents/rc_pc_pccs_doc_20020228_church-internet_en.html.

———. "Ethics in Internet." Vatican, February 22, 2002. www.vatican.varoman_curia/pontifical_councils/pccs/documents/rc_pc_pccs_doc_20020228_ethics-internet_en.html.

Postman, N. *Technopoly: The Surrender of Culture to Technology*. New York: Vintage Books, 1993.

Prisco, Giulio. "Virtual Reality a New Frontier for Religions." *Hypergrid Business*, February 29, 2015. www.hypergridbusiness.com/2015/02/virtual-reality-a-new-frontier-for-religions/.

Pullinger, D. *Information Technology and Cyberspace: Extra-Connected Living*. London: Darton, Longman and Todd, 2001.

Raine, Lee, and Barry Wellman. *Networked: The New Social Operating System*. Cambridge, MA: MIT Press, 2012.

Reid, E. "Virtual Worlds: Culture and Imagination." In *CyberSociety*, edited by S. Jones, 164–83. Thousand Oaks, CA: Sage, 1995.

Rheingold, H. *Smart Mobs: The Next Social Revolution*. Boston: Perseus Books, 2002.

Roncace, M., and P. Gray. *Teaching the Bible: Practical Strategies for Classroom Instruction*. Atlanta: Society of Biblical Literature, 2005.

Russell, R. J. "Five Attitudes toward Nature and Technology from a Christian Perspective." *Theology and Science* 1, no. 2 (2003): 149–59.

Salus, Peter H. *Casting the Net: From ARPANET to Internet and Beyond*. Reading, MA: Addison-Wesley, 1995.

Sanderson, J., and P. H. Cheong. "Tweeting Prayers and Communicating Grief over Michael Jackson Online." *Bulletin of Science, Technology & Society* 30, no. 5 (2010): 328–40.

Schroeder, R., N. Heather, and R. M. Lee. "The Sacred and the Virtual: Religion in Multi-User Virtual Reality." *Journal of Computer Mediated Communication* 4, no. 1 (1998). http://onlinelibrary.wiley.com/doi/10.1111/j.1083-6101.1998.tb00092.x/full.

Schultze, Q. *Habits of the High-Tech Heart*. Grand Rapids: Baker Academic, 2002.

———. *Redeeming Television: How TV Changes Christians—How Christians Can Change TV*. Downers Grove, IL: InterVarsity, 1992.

Silverstone, R., E. Hirsch, and D. Morley. "Information and Communication Technologies and the Moral Economy of the Household." In *Consuming Technologies: Media and Information in Domestic Spaces*, edited by R. Silverstone and E. Hirsch, 15–31. London: Routledge, 1992.

Sloop, John M., and Joshua Gunn. "Status Control: An Admonition Concerning the Publicized Privacy of Social Networking." *The Communication Review* 13, no. 4 (2010): 289–308.

Smith, C. *Soul Searching: The Religious and Spiritual Lives of American Teenagers*. New York: Oxford University Press, 2009.

Smith, G. V. *Hosea, Amos, Micah*. Grand Rapids: Zondervan, 2001.

Smith, T. L. "Darkness Is My Closest Friend: Using the Psalms of Lament to Address Grief Issues." Paper presented at NACSW Convention 2007, Dallas, March 2007. www.nacsw.org/Publications/Proceedings2007/SmithTDarkeness ClosestFriendE.pdf.

Society, Religion and Technology Project. "Bridging the Digital Divide." The Church of Scotland. December 18, 2014. www.srtp.org.uk/srtp/view_article /bridging_the_digital_divide.

Stackhouse, M. L. "Civil Religion, Political Theology and Public Theology: What's the Difference?" *Political Theology* 5, no. 3 (2004): 275–93.

Stoddart, E. "Who Watches the Watchers? Towards an Ethic of Surveillance in a Digital Age." *Studies in Christian Ethics* 21, no. 3 (2008): 362–81.

Synod of Bishops. *Justice in the World*. Spring Hill College. www.shc.edu/theo library/resources/synodjw.htm.

Tanner, K. "The Difference Theological Anthropology Makes." *Theology Today* 50, no. 4 (1994): 567–79.

Taylor, S. "Co-authoring Christianity." *Stimulus* 12, no. 3 (2004): 10–15.

———. *The Out of Bounds Church? Learning to Create a Community of Faith in a Culture of Change*. El Cajon, CA: Emergent YS; Grand Rapids: Zondervan, 2005.

———. "U2 and Public Lament for Pike River Miners." sustain.if.able kiwi (blog), November 26, 2010. www.emergentkiwi.org.nz/archive/u2-and -public-lament-for-pike-river-miners/.

Thompson, J. M. *Justice and Peace: A Christian Primer*. 2nd ed. Maryknoll, NY: Orbis Books, 2003.

Tillich, P. *Systematic Theology*. Vol. 1. Welwyn: James Nisbet, 1964.

Tönnies, F. *Community and Society*. East Lansing: Michigan State University Press, 1957.

Torma, Ryan, and Paul Emerson Teusner. "iReligion." *Studies in World Christianity* 17, no. 2 (2011): 137–55.

Tracy, D. *The Analogical Imagination: Christian Theology and the Culture of Pluralism*. New York: Crossroad, 1981.

Trueman, C. "What Do Miserable Christians Sing?" *Themelios* 25, no. 2 (2000): 1–3.

United Methodist Communications. "Group Email Netiquette." United Methodist Church. http://www.umcom.org/learn/social-media-etiquette-handbook.

van Dijk, Jan. *The Network Society*. Thousand Oaks, CA: Sage, 1999.

Vanhoozer, K. J. "What Is Everyday Theology? How and Why Christians Should Read Culture." In *Everyday Theology: How to Read Cultural Texts and Interpret Trends*, edited by K. J. Vanhoozer, C. A. Anderson, and M. J. Sleasman, 15–60. Grand Rapids: Baker Academic, 2007.

Volf, Miroslav. *After Our Likeness: The Church as the Image of the Trinity*. Grand Rapids: Eerdmans, 1998.

Volti, R. *Society and Technological Change*. 4th ed. New York: Worth, 2001.

Walsh, B. J., and S. Bouma-Prediger. "With and Without Boundaries: Christian Homemaking amidst Postmodern Homelessness." Christian Reformed Campus Ministries. http://crc.sa.utoronto.ca/articles/Boundaries.pdf.

Ward, P. *Liquid Church*. Peabody, MA: Hendrickson, 2002.

Wellman, B. "An Electronic Group Is Virtually a Social Network." In *Culture of the Internet*, edited by Sara Kiesler, 179–205. Mahwah, NJ: Lawrence Erlbaum Associates, 1997.

Wellman, B., and C. Haythornthwaite, eds. *The Internet in Everyday Life*. Oxford: Blackwell, 2002.

Wellman, B., and B. Leighton. "Networks, Neighborhoods and Communities: Approaches to the Study of the Community Question." *Urban Affairs Quarterly* 14 (1979): 363–90.

White, S. *Christian Worship and Technological Change*. Nashville: Abingdon, 1994.

White, S. J. *Groundwork of Christian Worship*. Peterborough, UK: Epworth, 1997.

Wilson, W. *The Internet Church*. Nashville: Word, 2000.

World Association for Christian Communication. *The No-Nonsense Guide to Citizen Journalism and Freedom of Expression*. Toronto: WACC, 2014.

Wright, C. J. H. *Living as the People of God: The Relevance of Old Testament Ethics*. Leicester, UK: Inter-Varsity, 1983.

Wyatt, Tim. "Plans Grow to Put WiFi in Every Church." *Church Times*, www.churchtimes.co.uk/articles/2015/9-january/news/uk/plans-grow-to-put-wifi-in-every-church.

Wynne-Jones, J. "Facebook and MySpace Can Lead Children to Commit Suicide, Warns Archbishop Nichols." *Daily Telegraph*, August 1, 2009. www.telegraph.co.uk/news/religion/5956719/Facebook-and-MySpace-can-lead-children-to-commit-suicide-warns-Archbishop-Nichols.html.

Yoder, P. *Shalom: The Bible's Word for Salvation, Justice, and Peace*. London: Spire, 1989.

Young, G. "Reading and Praying Online: The Continuity in Religion Online and Offline Religion in Internet Christianity." In *Religion Online: Finding Faith on the Internet*, edited by L. Dawson and D. Cowan, 93–106. New York: Routledge, 2004.

Zimmerman-Umble, D. "The Amish and the Telephone: Resistance and Reconstruction." In *Consuming Technologies: Media and Information in Domestic Spaces*, edited by R. Silverstone and E. Hirsch, 183–94. London: Routledge, 1992.

notes

Introduction

1. Barna Research Group, "Cyber Church: Pastors and the Internet," Barna Group, February 11, 2015, www.barna.org/barna-update/congregations/706-cyber-church-pastors-and-the-internet#.VVJbXcu9KSO. Jonathan Merritt, "Why Technology Didn't (and Won't) Destroy the Church," Religious News Service, February 27, 2015, http://jonathanmerritt.religionnews.com/2015/02/27/technology-hasnt-wont-destroy-church/.

2. Tim Wyatt, "Plans Grow to Put WiFi in Every Church," Church Times, January 9, 2015, www.churchtimes.co.uk/articles/2015/9-january/news/uk/plans-grow-to-put-wifi-in-every-church.

3. Tiffany Jothen, "6 Million Decisions for Christ Online. Many Receiving One-On-One Follow-Up." April 14, 2015, http://billygraham.org/story/6-million-decisions-for-christ-online-many-receiving-one-on-one-follow-up/.

4. "Global Media Outreach Exceeds Evangelism Goal," Global Media Outreach, January 23, 2014, www.globalmediaoutreach.com/blog/slug-jiw0a0.

5. Michael Gryboski, "A Holographic Bible? Microsoft Technology Offers 'Intriguing' Way for Future Bible Study," *Christian Post*, January 28, 2015, www.christianpost.com/news/a-holographic-bible-microsoft-technology-offers-intriguing-way-for-future-bible-study-133235/.

6. Giulio Prisco, "Virtual Reality a New Frontier for Religions," *Hypergrid Business*, February 9, 2015, www.hypergridbusiness.com/2015/02/virtual-reality-a-new-frontier-for-religions/.

7. Peter H. Salus, *Casting the Net: From ARPANET to Internet and Beyond* (Reading, MA: Addison-Wesley, 1995), 208.

8. Bill Gates, *The Road Ahead* (New York: Viking, 1995), 274.

9. Katie Hafner and Matthew Lyon, *Where Wizards Stay Up Late: Origins of the Internet* (New York: Simon & Schuster, 1996).

10. Steven G. Jones, "The Internet and Its Social Landscape," in *Virtual Culture: Identity and Communication in Cybersociety*, ed. Steven G. Jones (Thousand Oaks, CA: Sage, 1997), 22.

11. B. Wellman and B. Leighton, "Networks, Neighborhoods and Communities: Approaches to the Study of the Community Question," *Urban Affairs Quarterly* 14 (1979): 363–90.

12. B. Wellman, "An Electronic Group Is Virtually a Social Network," in *Culture of the Internet*, ed. Sara Kiesler (Mahwah, NJ: Lawrence Erlbaum Associates, 1997).

13. This view of community corresponds to Lev Manovich's description "new media," which we will discuss in chapter 2. See Lev Manovich, *The Language of New Media* (Cambridge, MA: MIT Press, 2001).

14. Jan van Dijk, *The Network Society* (Thousand Oaks, CA: Sage, 1999).

15. Manuel Castells, *The Rise of the Network Society*, vol. 1 of *The Information Age: Economy, Society and Culture*, 2nd ed. (Malden, MA: Blackwell, 2000).

16. Lee Raine and Barry Wellman, *Networked: The New Social Operating System* (Cambridge, MA: MIT Press), 2012.

17. Ibid., 9.

18. Ibid., 19.

19. While this may differ from traditional religious models and definitions of community, recent work on Christian community as a reflection of the Trinity shows that images of social relationships are flexible and adaptable and that we maintain bonds of commitment through dynamic interaction with one another and the divine. See Miroslav Volf, *After Our Likeness: The Church as the Image of the Trinity* (Grand Rapids: Eerdmans, 1998), and H. Campbell, *An Investigation of the Nature of Church through an Analysis of Christian Email-based Online Communities* (PhD diss., University of Edinburgh, 2001).

20. Nancy Ammerman, *Congregation and Community* (New Brunswick, NJ: Rutgers University Press, 1997).

21. Stephen Garner, "Theology and the New Media," in *Digital Religion: Understanding Religious Practice in New Media Worlds*, ed. Heidi Campbell (New York: Routledge, 2012).

22. Neil Darragh, *Doing Theology Ourselves: A Guide to Research and Action* (Auckland, NZ: Accent, 1995).

23. Ted Peters, *God—the World's Future: Systematic Theology for a New Era*, 2nd ed. (Minneapolis: Fortress, 2000), 7.

24. Stephen B. Bevans, *Models of Contextual Theology* (Maryknoll, NY: Orbis Books, 2002).

25. Kathryn Tanner, "The Difference Theological Anthropology Makes," *Theology Today* 50, no. 4 (1994): 567–68.

26. Quoted in Peters, *God*, 7.

27. Lesslie Newbigin, *Foolishness to the Greeks: The Gospel and Western Culture* (Grand Rapids: Eerdmans, 1986), 4.

28. Paul Tillich, *Systematic Theology*, vol. 1 (Welwyn, UK: James Nisbet, 1964), 67–73.

29. Stanley J. Grenz, *The Social God and the Relational Self: A Trinitarian Theology of the Imago Dei* (Louisville: Westminster John Knox, 2001), 8.

30. Christopher D. Marshall, *Kingdom Come: The Kingdom of God in the Teaching of Jesus* (Auckland: Bible College of New Zealand, 1990).

31. Dwight J. Friesen, *Thy Kingdom Connected: What the Church Can Learn from Facebook, the Internet, and Other Networks* (Grand Rapids: Baker Books, 2009), 43.

32. Ibid., 43–44.

33. Paul G. Hiebert, "Conversion, Culture and Cognitive Categories," *Gospel in Context* 1, no. 4 (1978); Dave Andrews, *Christi-Anarchy: Discovering a Radical Spirituality of Compassion* (Oxford: Lion, 1999); Friesen, *Thy Kingdom Connected*, 163–70.

Chapter 1 Theology of Technology 101

1. R. Volti, *Society and Technological Change*, 4th ed. (New York: Worth Publishers, 2001).

2. D. H. Hopper, *Technology, Theology, and the Idea of Progress* (Louisville: Westminster John Knox, 1991).

3. D. Pullinger, *Information Technology and Cyberspace: Extra-connected Living* (London: Darton, Longman and Todd, 2001).

4. P. Horsfield, "Media," in *Key Words in Religion, Media and Culture*, ed. D. Morgan (New York: Routledge, 2008), 111–22.

5. S. White, *Christian Worship and Technological Change* (Nashville: Abingdon, 1994).

6. Ibid., 16.

7. I. G. Barbour, *Ethics in an Age of Technology: The Gifford Lectures 1989–1991*, vol. 2 (San Francisco: HarperSanFrancisco, 1993), 3–4.

8. Volti, *Society and Technological Change*, 6.

9. K. Kelly, "The Third Culture," *Science* 279 (1998): 992–93.

10. Horsfield, "Media."

11. Ibid., 113.

12. S. V. Monsma, *Responsible Technology: A Christian Perspective* (Grand Rapids: Eerdmans, 1986), 13–20.

13. Ibid.

14. Ibid., 19.

15. P. Horsfield and K. Asamoah-Gyadu, "What Is It about the Book? Semantic and Material Dimensions in the Mediation of the Word of God," *Studies in World Christianity* 17, no. 2 (2011): 175–93; P. G. Horsfield, *The Mediated Spirit*, Commission for Mission, Uniting the Church in Australia, Melbourne, Australia: Synod of Victoria, 2002. CD-ROM.

16. Horsfield, *Mediated Spirit*.

17. Horsfield and Asamoah-Gyadu, "What Is It about the Book?," 182.

18. Ibid.; Horsfield, *Mediated Spirit*.

19. P. G. Horsfield and P. Teusner, "A Mediated Religion: Historical Perspectives on Christianity and the Internet," *Studies in World Christianity* 13, no. 3 (2007): 278–95.

20. Horsfield, *Mediated Spirit*.

21. Horsfield and Teusner, "A Mediated Religion," 282–84.

22. R. Cole-Turner, "Technology and the Mission of Theology in a New Century," in *God and Globalization: The Spirit and the Modern Authorities*, vol. 2, ed. M. L. Stackhouse and D. S. Browning (Harrisburg, PA: Trinity Press International, 2001), 139–65.

23. J. C. Briggs, "Bacon's Science and Religion," in *The Cambridge Companion to Bacon*, ed. M. Peltonen (Cambridge: Cambridge University Press, 1996), 172–99.

24. Francis Bacon et al., "The New Organon," in *The Works of Francis Bacon*, ed. F. Bacon, J. Spedding, R. L. Ellis, and D. D. Heath (London: Longman, 1857), 4:115.

25. C. Mitcham and J. Grote, "Aspects of Christian Exegesis: Hermeneutics, the Theological Virtues, and Technology," in *Theology and Technology: Essays in Christian Analysis and Exegesis*, ed. C. Mitcham and J. Grote (Lanham, MD: University Press of America, 1984), 33.

26. Horsfield, *Mediated Spirit*.

27. Ibid.

28. Stewart M. Hoover, *Religion in the Media Age* (New York: Routledge, 2006), 47–48.

29. Ibid., 227.

30. H. R. Niebuhr, *Christ and Culture* (New York: Harper, 1951).

31. Barbour, *Ethics*, 19.

32. Mitcham and Grote, "Aspects of Christian Exegesis, " 33; D. F. Noble, *The Religion of Technology: The Divinity of Man and the Spirit of Invention* (New York: Alfred A. Knopf, 1997), 48–53.

33. G. Houston, *Virtual Morality: Christian Ethics in the Computer Age* (Leicester, UK: Apollos, 1998).

34. Barbour, *Ethics*, 11.

35. Pullinger, *Information Technology*, 34.

36. J. Ellul, *The Technological Society* (New York: Vintage Books, 1964), xxv.

37. J. Wynne-Jones, "Facebook and MySpace Can Lead Children to Commit Suicide, Warns Archbishop Nichols," *Daily Telegraph*, August 1, 2009, www.telegraph.co.uk/news/religion/5956719/Facebook-and-MySpace-can-lead-children-to-commit-suicide-warns-Archbishop-Nichols.html.

38. Pontifical Council for Social Communications, "Ethics in Internet," Vatican, February 22, 2002, www.vatican.varoman_curia/pontifical_councils/pccs/documents/rc_pc_pccs_doc_20020228_ethics-internet_en.html.

39. Ibid.

40. C. J. Gardner, "Tangled in the Worst of the Web: What Internet Porn Did to One Pastor, His Wife, His Ministry, Their Life," *Christianity Today* 45, no. 4 (2001): 42–49.

41. Barbour, *Ethics*, 14–15.

42. Cole-Turner, "Technology and the Mission," 161.

43. Barbour, *Ethics*, 8–11.

44. Pontifical Council for Social Communications, "The Church and Internet," Vatican, February 22, 2002, www.vatican.va/roman_curia/pontifical_councils/pccs/documents/rc_pc_pccs_doc_20020228_church-internet_en.html.

45. Barbour, *Ethics*, 19.

46. R. Cole-Turner, *The New Genesis: Theology and the Genetic Revolution* (Louisville: Westminster John Knox, 1993), 102.

47. Monsma, *Responsible Technology*, 1.

48. B. A. Nardi and V. O'Day, *Information Ecologies: Using Technology with Heart* (Cambridge, MA: MIT Press, 1999), 49.

49. Ibid.

50. Stephen B. Bevans, *Models of Contextual Theology* (Maryknoll, NY: Orbis Books, 2002), 3–9.

51. L. Manovich, "New Media from Borges to HTML," *The New Media Reader* (2003): 13–28.

52. Nardi and O'Day, *Information Ecologies*, 50–56.

Chapter 2 New Media Theory 101

1. Lev Manovich, *The Language of New Media* (Cambridge, MA: MIT Press, 2001).

2. Ibid., 134.

3. D. Beer and R. Burrows, "Sociology and, of and in Web 2.0: Some Initial Considerations," *Sociological Research Online* 12, no. 5, www.socresonline.org.uk/12/5/17.html.

4. Manovich, *Language of New Media*, 209.

5. Ibid., 208–9.

6. Ibid., 230.

7. Ibid., 55–60.

8. Ibid., 134.

9. B. Wellman and C. Haythornthwaite, eds., *The Internet in Everyday Life* (Oxford: Blackwell, 2002).

10. H. Rheingold, *Smart Mobs: The Next Social Revolution* (Boston: Perseus Books, 2002), 195.

11. Jan van Djik, *The Network Society* (Thousand Oaks, CA: Sage, 1999).

12. John M. Sloop and Joshua Gunn, "Status Control: An Admonition Concerning the Publicized Privacy of Social Networking," *The Communication Review* 13, no. 4 (2010): 292.

13. This process is explored more in chapters 5 and 6 as we move toward thinking about what a theology of new media could look like.

Chapter 3 Networked Religion

1. See H. Campbell, "The Rise of the Study of Digital Religion," in *Digital Religion: Understanding Religious Practice in the New Media World* (London: Routledge, 2013), 1–22.

2. The concept of networked religion was first introduced in H. Campbell, "Understanding the Relationship between Religious Practice Online and Offline in a Networked Society," *Journal of the American Academy of Religion* 80, no. 1 (2012): 64–93.

3. H. Campbell, *When Religion Meets New Media* (London: Routledge, 2010), 123–25.

4. T. Hutchings, "Creating Church Online: Five Ethnographic Case Studies of Online Christian Community" (PhD diss., Durham University, 2010).

5. N. Baym, "The Emergence of Community in Computer-Mediated Communication," in *CyberSociety*, ed. S. Jones (Thousand Oaks, CA: Sage, 1995), 138–63; E. Reid, "Virtual Worlds: Culture and Imagination," in *CyberSociety*, ed. S. Jones (Thousand Oaks, CA: Sage, 1995), 164–83.

6. P. Kollock and M. Smith, "Managing the Virtual Commons: Cooperation and Conflict in Computer Communities," in *Computer-Mediated Communication: Linguistic, Social, and Cross-Cultural Perspectives*, ed. S. Herring (Amsterdam: J. Benjamins, 1994), 110–28.

7. Hutchings, "Creating Church Online."

8. H. Campbell, *Exploring Religious Community Online: We Are One in the Network* (New York: Peter Lang, 2005), 176–78.

9. G. Young, "Reading and Praying Online: The Continuity in Religion Online and Offline Religion in Internet Christianity," in *Religion Online—Finding Faith on the Internet*, ed. L. L. Dawson and D. E. Cowan (New York: Routledge, 2004), 93–106.

10. C. Smith, *Soul Searching: The Religious and Spiritual Lives of American Teenagers* (New York: Oxford University Press, 2009).

11. P. H. Cheong, A. Halavais, and K. Kwon, "The Chronicles of Me: Understanding Blogging as a Religious Practice," *Journal of Media and Religion* 7, no. 3 (2008): 107–31; H. Campbell, "Bloggers and Religious Authority Online," *Journal of Computer-Mediated Communication* 15, no. 2 (2010b): 251–76.

12. M. Lövheim, *Intersecting Identities: Young People, Religion and Interaction on the Internet* (Uppsala, Sweden: Uppsala University, 2004).

13. L. L. Dawson and J. Hennebry, "New Religions and the Internet: Recruiting in a New Public Space," in *Religion Online—Finding Faith on the Internet*, ed. L. L. Dawson and D. E. Cowan, 151–73.

14. Lövheim, *Intersecting Identities*, 50–55.

15. L. S. Clark, "Spirituality Online: Teen Friendship Circles and the Internet" (paper presented at the Fourth International Conference on Media, Religion and Culture, Louisville, September 1–4, 2004).

16. N. K. Baym, "The Emergence of On-Line Community," in *CyberSociety 2.0: Revisiting Computer-Mediated Community and Communication*, ed. S. G. Jones (Thousand Oaks, CA: Sage, 1998), 35–68.

17. B. Burkhalter, "Reading Race Online: Discovering Racial Identity in Usenet Discussions," in *Communities in Cyberspace*, ed. M. A. Smith and P. Kollock (London: Routledge, 1999), 60–75.

18. N. Elias and D. Lemish, "Spinning the Web of Identity: The Roles of the Internet in the Lives of Immigrant Adolescents," *New Media & Society* 11, no. 4 (2009): 533–51.

19. S. O'Leary and B. Brasher, "The Unknown God of the Internet," in *Philosophical Perspectives on Computer-Mediated Communication*, ed. C. Ess (Albany: State University of New York Press, 1996).

20. R. Schroeder, N. Heather, and R. M. Lee, "The Sacred and the Virtual: Religion in Multi-User Virtual Reality," *Journal of Computer-Mediated Communication* 4, no. 1 (1998), http://onlinelibrary.wiley.com/doi/10.1111/j.1083-6101.1998.tb00092.x/full.

21. B. Brasher, *Give Me That Online Religion* (San Francisco: Jossey-Bass, 2001).

22. Young, "Reading and Praying Online."

23. C. Helland, "Canadian Religious Diversity Online: A Network of Possibilities," in *Religion and Diversity in Canada*, ed. P. Beyer and L. Beaman (Boston: Brill, 2008), 127–48.

24. R. Bennett and H. Campbell, "Modern-Day Martyrs: Fans' Online Reconstruction of Celebrities as Divine," in *Social Media, Religion and Spirituality*, ed. D. Herbert and M. Gillispe (Berlin: De Gruyter, 2014).

25. J. Sanderson and P. H. Cheong, "Tweeting Prayers and Communicating Grief over Michael Jackson Online," *Bulletin of Science, Technology & Society* 30, no. 5 (2010): 328–40.

26. O. Krueger, "The Internet as a Mirror and Distributor of Religious and Ritual Knowledge," *Asian Journal of Social Sciences* 32, no. 2 (2004): 183–97.

27. L. Raine and B. Wellman, *Networked: The New Social Operating System* (Cambridge, MA: MIT Press, 2012).

28. G. G. Armfield and R. L. Holbert, "The Relationship between Religiosity and Internet Use," *Journal of Media and Religion* 3, no. 2 (2003): 139.

29. D. Herring, "Virtual as Contextual: A Net News Theology," in *Religion and Cyberspace*, ed. L. Dawson and D. Cowan (London: Routledge, 2005), 149–65.

30. H. Campbell, "Bloggers and Religious Authority Online," *Journal of Computer-Mediated Communication* 15, no. 2 (2010): 251–76.

31. Campbell, *When Religion Meets New Media*, 96–111.

32. Ibid., 140.

33. Ibid., 141.

34. P. H. Cheong and J. P. H. Poon, "Weaving Webs of Faith: Examining Internet Use and Religious Communication among Chinese Protestant Transmigrants," *Journal of International and Intercultural Communication* 2, no. 3 (2009): 189–207.

35. S. Jacobs, "Virtually Sacred: The Performance of Asynchronous Cyber-Rituals in Online Spaces," *Journal of Computer-Mediated Communication* 12, no. 3 (2007), 103–21; S. Jenkins, "Rituals and Pixels: Experiments in Online Church," *Heidelberg Journal of Religions on the Internet* 3, no. 1 (2008), http://archiv.ub.uniheidelberg.de/volltextserver/volltexte/2008/8291/pdf/jenkins.pdf.

36. Campbell, *When Religion Meets New Media*, 64–88.

37. B. Wellman and C. Haythornwaite, eds., *The Internet in Everyday Life* (Oxford: Blackwell, 2002), 12.

38. J. Katz and R. Rice, *Social Consequences of Internet Use: Access Involvement and Interaction* (Cambridge, MA: MIT Press, 2002); H. Campbell, "Challenges Created by Online Religious Networks," *Journal of Media and Religion* 3, no. 2 (2004), 81–99.

39. A. Kavanagh and S. Patterson, "The Impact of Community Computer Networks on Social Capital and Community Involvement in Blacksburg," in Wellman and Haythornthwaite, eds., *The Internet in Everyday Life*, 325–44.

40. R. Kraut et al., "Internet Paradox: A Social Technology That Reduces Social Involvement and Psychological Well-Being?," *American Psychologist* 53 (1998): 1017–19.

41. M. Bakardjieva, "Internet in Everyday Life: Exploring the Tenets and Contributions of Diverse Approaches," in *The Handbook of Internet Studies*, ed. C. Ess and M. Consalvo (Oxford: Blackwell, 2011), 59–82; H. Campbell and M. Lövheim, "Studying the Online-Offline Connection in Religion Online," *Information, Communication & Society* 14, no. 8 (2011): 1083–96.

42. C. Ess and M. Consalvo, "Introduction: What Is Internet Studies?" in *The Handbook of Internet Studies*, ed. C. Ess and M. Consalvo (Oxford: Blackwell, 2011), 1–8.

Chapter 4 Merging the Network with Theology

1. John Nolland, *Luke 9:21–18:34*, Word Biblical Commentary 35B (Dallas: Word Books, 1993).

2. Lynne M. Baab, *Friending: Real Relationships in a Virtual World* (Downers Grove, IL: InterVarsity, 2011), 11.

3. Daniel L. Migliore, *Faith Seeking Understanding: An Introduction to Christian Theology*, 2nd ed. (Grand Rapids: Eerdmans, 2004), 160.

4. Stanley J. Grenz, *Theology for the Community of God* (Carlisle: Paternoster, 1994), 85–88, 93; Karl Rahner, *The Trinity* (New York: Herder and Herder, 1970).

5. M. Jinkins, *Invitation to Theology: A Guide to Study, Conversation and Practice* (Downers Grove, IL: InterVarsity), 2001.

6. Christopher J. H. Wright, *Living as the People of God: The Relevance of Old Testament Ethics* (Leicester, UK: Inter-Varsity, 1983), 133–47.

7. See "LifeGroups," Life.Church, www.life.church/lifegroups/.

8. Pontifical Council for Social Communications, "The Church and Internet," Vatican, February 22, 2002, www.vatican.va/roman_curia/pontifical_councils/pccs/documents/rc_pc_pccs_doc_20020228_church-internet_en.html.

9. T. Hutchings, "Creating Church Online: Five Ethnographic Case Studies of Online Christian Community" (PhD diss., Durham University, 2010); Mission and Public Affairs Council, *Mission-Shaped Church: Church Planting and Fresh Expressions of Church in a Changing Context* (London: Church House, 2004).

10. Christopher Helland, "Online-Religion/Religion-Online and Virtual Communitas," in *Religion on the Internet: Research Prospects and Promises*, ed. Douglas E. Cowan and Jeffrey K. Hadden (New York: JAI, 2000), 205–23.

11. Dwight J. Friesen, *Thy Kingdom Connected: What the Church Can Learn from Facebook, the Internet, and Other Networks* (Grand Rapids: Baker Books, 2009), 112–17.

12. Kester Brewin, *The Complex Christ: Signs of Emergence in the Urban Church* (London: SPCK, 2004), 82–85.

13. S. White, *Christian Worship and Technological Change* (Nashville: Abingdon, 1994), 118–19.

14. Katharine Sarah Moody, "Researching Theo(b)logy: Emerging Christian Communities and the Internet," in *Exploring Religion and the Sacred in a Media Age*, ed. Christopher Deacy and Elisabeth Arweck (Farnham, UK: Ashgate, 2009), 242–43.

15. Tim Bednar, "Blogging: Report from a Grassroots Revival," *Stimulus* 12, no. 3 (2004): 28.

16. P. G. Horsfield and P. Teusner, "A Mediated Religion: Historical Perspectives on Christianity and the Internet," *Studies in World Christianity* 13, no. 3 (2007): 278–95.

17. Philip R. Meadows, "The Gospel in Cyberspace: Reflections on Virtual Reality," *Epworth Review* 22 (1995): 53–73.

18. José Miguez Bonino, *Room to Be People: An Interpretation of the Message of the Bible for Today's World*, trans. Vickie Leach (Geneva: World Council of Churches, 1975), 31–33.

19. Gustavo Gutiérrez, *A Theology of Liberation*, trans. Sister Caridad Inda and John Eagleson (London: SCM, 1974), 294–95.

20. Simon Carey Holt, *God Next Door: Spirituality and Mission in the Neighbourhood* (Brunswick East, Australia: Acorn Press, 2007).

21. Ibid., 77.

22. Brian J. Walsh and Steven Bouma-Prediger, "With and Without Boundaries: Christian Homemaking amidst Postmodern Homelessness," http://crc.sa.utoronto.ca/files/2010/01/with-and-without-boundaries.pdf.

23. Christopher D. Marshall, *Compassionate Justice: An Interdisciplinary Dialogue with Two Gospel Parables on Law, Crime, and Restorative Justice* (Eugene, OR: Cascade Books, 2012), 120.

24. Ibid., 127–28.

25. Holt, *God Next Door*, 83.

26. B. Brasher, *Give Me That Online Religion* (San Francisco: Jossey-Bass, 2001), 152.

27. K. Kelly, "Nerd Theology," *Technology in Society* 21, no. 4 (1999): 387–92.

28. Holt, *God Next Door*, 83.

29. David Lyon, "Would God Use Email?," *Zadok Perspectives* 71 (2001): 20–23.

30. Pontifical Council for Social Communications, "Ethics in Internet," Vatican, February 28, 2002, www.vatican.varoman_curia/pontifical_councils/pccs/documents/rc_pc_pccs_doc_20020228_ethics-internet_en.html.

31. Nicola David, *Staying Safe Online* (Cambridge: Grove Books, 2007); Christine J. Gardner, "Tangled in the Worst of the Web: What Internet Porn Did to One Pastor, His Wife, His Ministry, Their Life," *Christianity Today* 45, no. 4 (2001): 42–49; Lynne M. Baab, *Reaching Out in a Networked World: Expressing Your Congregation's Heart and Soul* (Herndon, VA: Alban Institute, 2008).

32. Meadows, "Gospel in Cyberspace," 53–73.

33. G. Houston, *Virtual Morality: Christian Ethics in the Computer Age* (Leicester, UK: Apollos, 1998).

34. Eric Stoddart, "Who Watches the Watchers? Towards an Ethic of Surveillance in a Digital Age," *Studies in Christian Ethics* 21, no. 3 (2008): 362–81.

35. David Clough, "The Message of the Medium: The Challenge of the Internet to the Church and Other Communities," *Studies in Christian Ethics* 13, no. 2 (2000): 91–100.

36. Caritas Aotearoa New Zealand, *The Digital Divide: Poverty and Wealth in the Information Age*, Social Justice Series (Wellington: Caritas Aotearoa New Zealand, 2000); John Ottmar, "Cyberethics: New Challenges or Old Problems," *Concilium*, no. 1 (2005); Pontifical Council for Social Communications, "Ethics in Internet."

Chapter 5 Developing a Faith-Based Community Response to New Media

1. H. Campbell, *When Religion Meets New Media* (London: Routledge, 2010), 41–63.

2. Ibid.

3. J. Ferre, "The Media of Popular Piety," in *Mediating Religion: Conversation in Media, Religion and Culture*, ed. J. Mitchell and S. Marriage (London: T&T Clark, 2003), 83–92.

4. A. Careaga, *E-vangelism: Sharing the Gospel in Cyberspace* (Lafayette, LA: Huntington, 1999); W. Wilson, *The Internet Church* (Nashville: Word, 2000).

5. J. Ellul, *The Technological Society* (New York: Vintage Books, 1964).

6. Q. Schultze, *Redeeming Television: How TV Changes Christians—How Christians Can Change TV* (Downers Grove, IL: InterVarsity, 1992).

7. Q. Schultze, *Habits of the High-Tech Heart* (Grand Rapids: Baker Academic, 2002).

8. Ferre, "Media of Popular Piety," 89.

9. Campbell, *When Religion Meets New Media*.

10. R. Silverstone, E. Hirsch, and D. Morley, "Information and Communication Technologies and the Moral Economy of the Household," in *Consuming Technologies: Media and Information in Domestic Spaces*, ed. R. Silverstone and E. Hirsch (London: Routledge, 1992), 15–31.

11. D. Zimmerman-Umble, "The Amish and the Telephone: Resistance and Reconstruction," in *Consuming Technologies*, 183–94.

12. Campbell, *When Religion Meets New Media*.

13. See Brian Ries, "Priests Share #ashtag Selfies in Observance of Ash Wednesday," Mashable, February 18, 2015, http://mashable.com/2015/02/18/priests-ashtag-selfies-ash-wednesday/.

14. Pontifical Council for Social Communications, "The Church and Internet," Vatican, February 22, 2002, www.vatican.va/roman_curia/pontifical_councils/pccs/documents/rc_pc_pccs_doc_20020228_church-internet_en.html; Pontifical Council for Social Communications, "Ethics in Internet," Vatican, February 22, 2002, www.vatican.va/roman_curia/pontifical_councils/pccs/documents/rc_pc_pccs_doc_20020228_ethics-internet_en.html.

Chapter 6 Engaging Appropriately with Technology and Media

1. Stanley J. Grenz, *The Moral Quest: Foundations of Christian Ethics* (Leicester, UK: Apollos, 1997).

2. Duncan B. Forrester, "The Scope of Public Theology," *Studies in Christian Ethics* 17, no. 2 (2004): 6.

3. Paul Tillich, *Systematic Theology*, vol. 1 (Welwyn, UK: James Nisbet, 1964), 67–73.

4. Max L. Stackhouse, "Civil Religion, Political Theology and Public Theology: What's the Difference?," *Political Theology* 5, no. 3 (2004): 275–93.

5. Chris Marshall, "What Language Shall I Borrow? The Bilingual Dilemma of Public Theology," *Stimulus* 13, no. 3 (2005): 11–18.

6. Kathryn Tanner, "The Difference Theological Anthropology Makes," *Theology Today* 50, no. 4 (1994): 567–79.

7. Marshall, "What Language," 11–18.

8. David Tracy, *The Analogical Imagination: Christian Theology and the Culture of Pluralism* (New York: Crossroad, 1981), 5.

9. Elaine L. Graham, Heather Walton, and Frances Ward, *Theological Reflection: Methods* (London: SCM Press, 2005), 159–61.

10. Ibid., 138–40.

11. Stackhouse, "Civil Religion, Political Theology and Public Theology," 291.

12. Douglas John Hall, *Professing the Faith: Christian Theology in a North American Context* (Minneapolis: Fortress, 1993), 33.

13. H. Campbell, *When Religion Meets New Media* (London: Routledge, 2010).

14. Marshall, "What Language," 11–18.

15. Ibid.; Robert Gascoigne, *The Public Forum and Christian Ethics* (Cambridge: Cambridge University Press, 2001).

16. I. G. Barbour, *Ethics in an Age of Technology: The Gifford Lectures 1989–1991*, vol. 2 (San Francisco: HarperSanFrancisco, 1993), 25.

17. B. A. Nardi and V. O'Day, *Information Ecologies: Using Technology with Heart* (Cambridge, MA: MIT Press, 1999).

18. Darrell L. Bock, *Luke*, NIV Application Commentary (Grand Rapids: Zondervan, 1996), 134–35.

19. Walter Brueggemann, "Voices of the Night—Against Justice," in *To Act Justly, Love Tenderly, Walk Humbly: An Agenda for Ministers*, ed. Walter Brueggemann, Sharon Daloz Parks, and Thomas H. Groome (New York: Paulist Press, 1986), 5–28.

20. Christopher J. H. Wright, *Living as the People of God: The Relevance of Old Testament Ethics* (Leicester, UK: Inter-Varsity, 1983), 133–47.

21. Duncan B. Forrester, "Social Justice and Welfare," in *The Cambridge Companion to Christian Ethics*, ed. Robin Gill (Cambridge: Cambridge University Press, 2001), 197.

22. D. A. Baer and R. P. Gordon, "Hesed," in *The New International Dictionary of Old Testament Theology and Exegesis*, ed. Willem VanGemeren (Grand Rapids: Zondervan, 1997), 211–18.

23. Gary V. Smith, *Hosea/Amos/Micah*, NIV Application Commentary (Grand Rapids: Zondervan, 2001), 554.

24. Perry Yoder, *Shalom: The Bible's Word for Salvation, Justice & Peace* (London: Spire, 1989), 10–19.

25. Robert J. Russell, "Five Attitudes toward Nature and Technology from a Christian Perspective," *Theology and Science* 1, no. 2 (2003): 157.

26. Synod of Bishops, "Justice in the World" (1971), para. 6.

27. Joseph Milburn Thompson, *Justice and Peace: A Christian Primer*, 2nd ed. (Maryknoll, NY: Orbis Books, 2003), 193–99.

28. Forrester, "Social Justice and Welfare," 195–96.

29. T. Hartley Hall IV, "The Shape of Reformed Piety," in *Spiritual Traditions for the Contemporary Church*, ed. Robin Maas and Gabriel O'Donnell (Nashville: Abingdon, 1990), 202–21.

30. Wright, *Living as the People of God*, 133–47.

31. Forrester, "Social Justice and Welfare," 198.

32. D. B. Forrester, *Christian Justice and Public Policy* (Cambridge: Cambridge University Press, 1997), 247.

33. Chris Arthur and World Association for Christian Communication, *Religion and the Media: An Introductory Reader* (Cardiff: University of Wales Press, 1993); World Association for Christian Communication, *The No-Nonsense Guide to Citizen Journalism and Freedom of Expression* (Toronto: WACC, 2014).

34. Lester Meriwether, "35 Ways Your Church Can Promote Adult and Family Literacy in Your Community," *Texas Adult & Family Literacy Quarterly* 13, no. 2 (April 2009), http://www-tcall.tamu.edu/newsletr/apr09/apr09c.html; Religion and Technology Project Society, "Bridging the Digital Divide," The Church of Scotland, www.srtp.org.uk/srtp/view_article/bridging_the_digital_divide.

35. See Caritas Aotearoa New Zealand, *The Digital Divide: Poverty and Wealth in the Information Age*, Social Justice Series (Wellington: Caritas Aotearoa New Zealand, 2000); John Ottmar, "Cyberethics: New Challenges or Old Problems," *Concilium*, no. 1 (2005): 15–26; Pontifical Council for Social Communications, "The Church and Internet," Vatican, February 22, 2002, www.vatican.va/roman_curia/pontifical_councils/pccs/documents/rc_pc_pccs_doc_20020228_church-internet_en.html.

36. Eric Stoddart, "Who Watches the Watchers? Towards an Ethic of Surveillance in a Digital Age," *Studies in Christian Ethics* 21, no. 3 (2008): 362–81.

37. Steve Taylor, *The Out of Bounds Church? Learning to Create a Community of Faith in a Culture of Change* (El Cajon, CA: Emergent YS; Grand Rapids: Zondervan, 2005).

38. Ibid., 128–29.

39. Lynne M. Baab, *Friending: Real Relationships in a Virtual World* (Downers Grove, IL: InterVarsity, 2011).

40. Ibid., 48.

41. Pete Ward, *Liquid Church* (Peabody, MA: Hendrickson, 2002).

42. Tim Bednar, "Blogging: Report from a Grassroots Revival," *Stimulus* 12, no. 3 (2004): 24–30.

43. T. Hutchings, "Creating Church Online: Five Ethnographic Case Studies of Online Christian Community" (PhD diss., Durham University, 2010), 243–60.

44. Bill McKibben, *Enough: Staying Human in an Engineered Age* (New York: Times Books, 2003), 166–68.

45. Kevin D. Miller, "Technological Prudence: What the Amish Can Teach Us," *Christian Reflection: A Series in Faith and Ethics* (2011): 20–28.

46. Ibid., 22.

47. Ibid., 23.

48. Donald B. Kraybill, Steven M. Nolt, and David Weaver-Zercher, *The Amish Way: Patient Faith in a Perilous World* (San Francisco: Jossey-Bass, 2010).

49. Evangelical Environmental Network, "What Would Jesus Drive?," www.whatwouldjesus drive.info; Katherine Ellison, "Stopping Traffic: What Would Jesus Drive?," *Christian Century* 119, no. 24 (2002): 8; Christine McMorris, "What Would Jesus Drive?," *Religion in the News* 6, no. 1 (2003): 19–21; Ryan Beiler, "Would Jesus Drive a Mercedes? The Untapped Potential of Biodiesel," *Sojourners* 35, no. 1 (2006): 9.

50. Susan J. White, *Groundwork of Christian Worship* (Peterborough: Epworth Press, 1997), 118–19.

51. Taylor, *Out of Bounds Church.*

52. Kevin J. Vanhoozer, "What Is Everyday Theology? How and Why Christians Should Read Culture," in *Everyday Theology: How to Read Cultural Texts and Interpret Trends*, ed. Kevin J. Vanhoozer, Charles A. Anderson, and Michael J. Sleasman (Grand Rapids: Baker Academic, 2007), 28–32.

53. Ryan Torma and Paul Emerson Teusner, "iReligion," *Studies in World Christianity* 17, no. 2 (2011): 153.

54. Eileen D. Crowley, *A Moving Word: Media Art in Worship*, Worship Matters (Minneapolis: Augsburg Fortess, 2006); Eileen D. Crowley, *Liturgical Art for a Media Culture*, American Essays in Liturgy (Collegeville, MN: Liturgical Press, 2007); Steve Taylor, "Co-authoring Christianity," *Stimulus* 12, no. 3 (2004): 10–15.

55. Philip Hefner, *The Human Factor: Evolution, Culture and Religion*, Theology and the Sciences (Minneapolis: Fortress, 1993); Philip Hefner, *Technology and Human Becoming* (Minneapolis: Fortress, 2003).

56. Presbyterian Youth Ministries, "Kiwi Easter," Presbyterian Church of Aotearoa New Zealand, www.facebook.com/kiwieaster.

57. "Christian Media," in *Media* 7 (New Zealand: TVNZ & Top Shelf Productions, April 5, 2012).

58. Stephen R. Garner, "Image-Bearing Cyborgs?," *Interface* 15, no. 1 (2011): 31–50.

59. Steve Collins, "Labyrinth," www.labyrinth.org.uk.

60. Carl Trueman, "What Do Miserable Christians Sing?," *Themelios* 25, no. 2 (2000): 1–3.

61. Mark Roncace and Patrick Gray, *Teaching the Bible: Practical Strategies for Classroom Instruction* (Atlanta: Society of Biblical Literature, 2005).

62. John Hammersley, "Psalm of Despair," www.psalmsoflife.com/psalm68.htm; Terry L. Smith, "Darkness Is My Closest Friend: Using the Psalms of Lament to Address Grief Issues" (paper presented at the NACSW Convention 2007, Dallas, March 2007), www.nacsw.org/Publications /Proceedings2007/SmithTDarkenessClosestFriendE.pdf.

63. Jonny Baker, "Worship Trick 71," jonnybaker (blog), February 15, 2004, http://jonnybaker .blogs.com/jonnybaker/2004/02/worship_trick_7.html.

64. NZPA, "U2 Pays Tribute to Lost Miners," Fairfax New Zealand, November 26, 2010, www.stuff.co.nz/entertainment/music/4392642/U2-pays-tribute-to-lost-miners.

65. Jetskifisher, "U2 Live in Auckland 25 Nov 2010—One Tree Hill in Memory of Westcaost Miners. R.I.P.," YouTube, www.youtube.com/watch?v=hMnycVi0zoU; kiwistu72, "U2—One Tree

Hill—Auckland 25 Nov 10—Dedicated to Our Lost Miners—May They RIP," YouTube, www.you tube.com/watch?v=2c1BLn7-bsY.

66. Steve Taylor, "U2 and Public Lament for Pike River Miners," sustain.if.able kiwi (blog), November 26, 2010, www.emergentkiwi.org.nz/archive/u2-and-public-lament-for-pike-river-miners/.

67. Elizabeth Boase and Steve Taylor, "Lament in an Age of New Media," in *Spiritual Complaint: Theology and Practice of Lament*, ed. Miriam J. Bier and Tim Bulkeley (Eugene, OR: Pickwick, 2013), 205–27.

index